Cryptocurrency

The Optimal Approaches For Forex And Crypto Trading.
The Process Of Generating Online Income Through
Forex Trading

*(Maximizing Returns In Decentralized Finance: An
Introduction To Defi And Profit Generation)*

Novica Scheiber

TABLE OF CONTENT

Cryptocurrency Exchanges

Numerous less prominent cryptocurrencies are solely traded via private, peer-to-peer transactions, consequently rendering them less liquid and presenting challenges in terms of valuation when compared to both other cryptocurrencies and fiat currencies.

Typical digital currencies, such as Bitcoin and Ripple, are exchanged on secondary markets that are closely linked to foreign exchange markets for traditional fiat currencies. (An illustration of this can be seen with the now obsolete Mt. Gox.) These platforms provide an avenue for individuals who possess cryptocurrencies to convert their assets into prominent fiat currencies such as the U.S. dollar and euro, as well as other less prevalent cryptocurrencies. In consideration of the services provided, they collect a modest portion of the financial value of each transaction – generally below 1%.

Cryptocurrency exchanges play a vital role in the creation of liquid markets for widely-used cryptocurrencies and in ascertaining their valuation in relation to traditional currencies. In contrast, the pricing of exchanges can exhibit significant variability. After the collapse of Mt. Gox, the value of bitcoin in relation to the U.S. dollar experienced a significant decline of over 50%. However, in the subsequent year of 2017, the exchange rate saw a remarkable surge of more than tenfold due to the exponential growth in demand for cryptocurrencies. Additionally, it is possible to engage in cryptocurrency futures trading on select cryptocurrency exchanges or closely monitor diversified cryptocurrency portfolios through the utilization of crypto indexes. This testimonial provided by the BBOD trader delves into extensive details regarding the practice of cryptocurrency trading.

The Development and Progression of Cryptocurrency

Prior to the emergence of the initial digital alternative currencies, cryptocurrency existed solely as a theoretical framework. Initial proponents of cryptocurrencies were driven by the objective of leveraging state-of-the-art mathematical and computer science concepts to tackle perceived functional and political shortcomings inherent in conventional fiat currencies.

TECHNICAL FOUNDATIONS

The origins of cryptocurrency can be attributed to the early 1980s, during which time David Chaum, an American cryptographer, pioneered the development of a "blinding" algorithm that is integral to the present-day web-based encryption systems. The algorithm facilitated the exchange of secure and immutable data, thus establishing the foundation for forthcoming electronic monetary transactions. This concept was commonly known as "blinded capital."

Chaum collaborated with a select group of cryptocurrency enthusiasts in the late 1980s to undertake the commercialization of the concept of blinded currency. Upon his arrival in the Netherlands, he established DigiCash, an enterprise, which developed monetary units by utilizing the blinding algorithm. DigiCash exhibited lack of decentralization in contrast to Bitcoin and majority of contemporary digital currencies. Chaum's company enjoyed an exclusive control over supply management, akin to the monopoly that central banks possess regarding fiat currencies.

DigiCash made initial attempts to engage in direct negotiations with individuals, however, the objection from the Dutch central bank resulted in the suspension of the proposal. In light of an impending deadline, DigiCash opted to exclusively offer its products to authorized banks, thereby significantly curtailing its market prospects. Subsequently, Microsoft initiated communication with DigiCash regarding a potentially advantageous partnership, which would have facilitated the ability of early Windows users to engage in transactions using DigiCash's currency. However, despite their efforts, the two companies failed to reach a mutually beneficial agreement, leading to the eventual closure of DigiCash in the late 1990s.

Approximately at the same period, Wei Dai, a highly respected professional in the field of software development, published a comprehensive document discussing the concept of b-money. This virtual currency framework incorporated numerous essential elements of contemporary cryptocurrencies, encompassing intricate privacy measures and decentralized structure. In contrast, B-money did not serve as a medium of exchange.

Soon after, an individual affiliated with Chaum named Nick Szabo developed and publicly released Bit Gold, a cryptocurrency that was remarkable for its utilization of blockchain technology, which serves as the contemporary bedrock for cryptocurrencies. Bit Gold, similar to DigiCash, did not attain widespread adoption and is currently obsolete as a means of conducting commerce.

PRE-BITCOIN VIRTUAL CURRENCIES

Subsequent to the emergence of DigiCash, a significant portion of research and investment in electronic financial transactions shifted towards conventional digital intermediaries, such as PayPal. This platform itself served as a precursor to the skyrocketing popularity of mobile payment technologies witnessed in the last decade. In various regions across the globe, there has been emergence of imitations of DigiCash, such as Russia's WebMoney.

During the late 1990s and early 2000s, E-gold emerged as the preeminent virtual currency within the United

States, gaining substantial recognition and prominence. The currency is developed and controlled by a company called e-gold, which is based in Florida. The company known as e-gold operated as a virtual platform for purchasing gold. Patrons, or individuals engaged in purchasing, sent their previous assortments of jewelry, small decorative items, and coins to the online repository of gold known as e-warehouse gold, in return for electronic "e-gold" – currency units denominated in gold. E-gold users have the option to exchange their stocks with other users, redeem them for physical gold, or convert their e-gold into U.S. dollars.

During its peak in the mid-2000s, E-gold boasted a substantial number of active accounts, reaching into the millions, and facilitated a sizeable volume of financial transactions amounting to billions of dollars on an annual basis. Regrettably, as a result of its inadequate security protocols, e-gold has emerged as a frequent target for cybercriminals and individuals engaged in fraudulent phishing activities, thereby exposing its users to potential monetary harm. In the mid-2000s, a considerable portion of the operations conducted by e-transaction gold had fallen into a legal grey area due to the company's insufficient legal enforcement protocols. This rendered it an attractive platform for illicit money laundering activities and the facilitation of small-scale Ponzi schemes. During the middle and later years of the 2000s, the website incurred growing legal investigation and subsequently ceased its operations in 2009.

The Contemporary Surge in Cryptocurrency and the Rise of Bitcoin

Bitcoin is widely regarded as the inaugural contemporary digital currency, owing to its pioneering synthesis of decentralized authority, user confidentiality, blockchain-driven ledger maintenance, and inherent scarcity in the realm of publicly utilized mediums of exchange. The concept was initially introduced by Satoshi

Nakamoto, an individual or collective entity who presented it through a white paper published in 2008.

In the beginning of 2009, the individual known as Satoshi Nakamoto introduced Bitcoin to the wider populace, consequently prompting a limited group of fervent advocates to engage in currency trading and mining activities. By the end of 2010, a plethora of comparable digital currencies, such as Litecoin and other widely adopted alternatives, had commenced their introduction to the market. Concurrently, the first public Bitcoin exchanges materialized.

WordPress was the pioneering retailer that commenced accepting Bitcoin payments in the latter part of 2012. Additional companies that adopted similar practices include Newegg.com, an e-commerce platform specializing in electronics, Expedia, a renowned travel booking website, and Microsoft, a leading technology corporation. A large number of merchants currently acknowledge the world's most renowned cryptocurrency as a legitimate means of exchange. Furthermore, there has been a rapid proliferation of innovative cryptocurrency applications, exemplified by Cryptomaniaks, which provides a detailed examination of the burgeoning realm of cryptocurrency-based sports betting platforms.

Despite the limited acceptance of cryptocurrencies other than Bitcoin for merchant payments, there is an increasing number of operational exchanges that facilitate the exchange of these cryptocurrencies for Bitcoin or traditional fiat currencies. This provides essential liquidity and flexibility to holders of cryptocurrencies. From the latter part of the 2010s onwards, significant corporations and institutional investors have maintained vigilant observation of what they term as the 'cryptocurrency void'.

BENEFITS OF CRYPTOCURRENCY

The majority of cryptocurrencies are created with the concept of scarcity being a central focus; the underlying source code establishes the ultimate limit on the quantity of units that can ever be in circulation. Cryptocurrencies can be compared to precious metals rather than traditional fiat currencies in this context. Similar to precious metals, they offer protection against inflation, which is not available to users of fiat currency.

Dismantling of Government Currency Monopolies

Cryptocurrencies provide a secure medium of exchange that is autonomous from established financial institutions like the Federal Reserve of the United States and the European Central Bank. This resonates with individuals who are apprehensive about the potential impact of quantitative easing (the process of central banks increasing the money supply by purchasing government bonds) and other lenient monetary policies, such as extremely low interbank lending rates, on fostering prolonged economic instability.

A widely held belief among economists and political scientists is that governments are likely to adopt cryptocurrency, or at the very least, incorporate certain elements of cryptocurrency into conventional currencies, such as incorporating traits like limited availability and enhanced security protocols. This mitigates the worries of certain advocates of cryptocurrency regarding the inflationary nature of fiat currencies and the inherent instability associated with physical cash.

Communities characterized by self-interest and self-regulation

In the realm of digital currencies, mining serves as an inherent mechanism for quality assurance and regulatory oversight. Given that miners are remunerated for their endeavors, they possess a vested financial stake in maintaining accurate and current transactional documentation. This guarantee supports the integrity of the system and upholds the value of the currency.

Robust Privacy Protections

Privacy and anonymity were significant concerns among early cryptocurrency proponents, and these concerns persist to this day. Numerous individuals who engage in cryptocurrency transactions employ fictitious names that have no correlation to their personal details, accounts, or stored information. Although experienced members of the community possess the ability to infer the identities of users, contemporary cryptocurrencies developed after Bitcoin have implemented supplementary measures that greatly amplify the level of complexity involved in doing so.

Authorities will encounter greater challenges in enforcing monetary retaliation.

In instances where individuals residing in authoritarian nations incur the disapproval of their governments, these governments possess the capability to promptly immobilize or appropriate their domestic bank accounts and undo transactions involving local currency. This issue is particularly disquieting in authoritarian nations such as China and Russia, where affluent individuals who incur the displeasure of the governing party frequently encounter profound monetary and legal challenges of dubious provenance.

Cryptocurrencies, in contrast to fiat currencies issued by central banks, exhibit a high degree of resilience against authoritarian whims. Implementing government regulations, while also accounting for global cooperation, is highly impractical due to the dispersed nature of cryptocurrency assets and transaction data across multiple international locations. It is an overstatement, but utilizing cryptocurrency is comparable to gaining access to a nearly boundless array of overseas financial institutions.

For governments with a history of relying on financial control methods or coercive tactics to maintain control over troublesome elites, the concept of decentralization presents a formidable challenge. In the latter part of 2017, CoinTelegraph released an article regarding a worldwide cryptocurrency initiative spearheaded by the Russian government. In the event of a successful implementation, this project would yield dual benefits to the stakeholders involved, specifically in terms of diminishing the dominant position of the US dollar as the global medium of exchange. It would provide participating governments with enhanced regulatory oversight over the expanding global reserves of valuable cryptocurrencies.

In the majority of instances, it is more cost-effective than conventional electronic transactions.

Blockchains, private keys, and wallets aptly tackle the issue of double-spending, thereby safeguarding emerging cryptocurrencies against potential exploitation by adept perpetrators who possess the ability to replicate digital assets. In addition, the security attributes of cryptocurrencies eliminate the necessity for a third-party payment processor, such as Visa or

PayPal, to verify and authorize electronic financial transactions.

Consequently, the imposition of compulsory transaction fees to support the efforts of payment processors is unnecessary, given that miners, who serve as the cryptocurrency counterparts to these processors, are already rewarded with newly generated currency units alongside optional transaction fees for their services. In contrast to the transaction fees of credit card payment processors and PayPal, which typically range from 1.5 percent to 3 percent, the fees associated with cryptocurrency transactions generally amount to less than 1 percent of the total transaction value.

Reduced Obstacles and Expenses in International Transactions.

In the realm of cryptocurrency, there is no distinction in the treatment of international transactions compared to domestic transactions. Irrespective of the geographical locations of the sender and receiver, transactions can be conducted without any charges or subject to a nominal transaction fee. This confers a substantial advantage in contrast to international transactions involving fiat currency, wherein additional charges are typically incurred that are not applicable to domestic transactions, such as fees associated with international credit cards or ATM usage. Currency exchanges between foreign parties can incur significant expenses due to high transaction fees, which can range from 10% to 15% of the total amount transferred.

Additionally, it is worth noting that numerous conventional credit cards impose international transaction fees, thereby substantially raising the expenses associated with conducting transactions in foreign nations.

CONS OF CRYPTOCURRENCY

Insufficient Regulation Encourages Illicit Trade

The capacity of cryptocurrency to facilitate illicit activities is arguably its most significant drawback and regulatory apprehension. Bitcoin and other cryptocurrencies are utilized in numerous transactions conducted within illicit online markets. Silk Road's infamous dark web platform leveraged Bitcoin to facilitate illicit drug transactions and engage in various illegal practices until its cessation in 2014. Cryptocurrencies are increasingly being employed for the illicit practice of money laundering, wherein unlawfully obtained funds are funneled through an intermediary that appears legitimate in order to obfuscate their source.

The very attributes that render cryptocurrencies challenging for governments to confiscate and surveil present a comparatively simplified avenue for illicit activities to transpire. However, it is important to acknowledge that the individual responsible for founding Silk Road is presently incarcerated due to a protracted investigation conducted by the DEA.

Potential for Tax Evasion in Certain Legal Jurisdictions

Cryptocurrencies possess inherent appeal to individuals engaging in tax evasion as they operate independently from national governments, existing beyond their direct influence. Numerous small enterprises resort to compensating their workforce in cryptocurrencies such as bitcoin, with the intention of evading payroll taxes and assisting their employees in circumventing income tax obligations. On the other hand, online merchants frequently adopt the use of cryptocurrencies as a means of circumventing the obligation to pay taxes on sales and earnings.

As per the official regulations outlined by the Internal Revenue Service (IRS), all transfers of cryptocurrency involving U.S. individuals and companies are subject to uniform taxation guidelines. However, several nations lack the implementation of such policies. Due to the intrinsic feature of anonymity associated with cryptocurrency, it poses challenges in effectively overseeing certain contraventions of tax laws, especially those related to pseudonymous internet merchants as opposed to employers who disclose an employee's actual name on a W-2 form, indicating their taxable bitcoin earnings for the fiscal year.

The Potentiality For Incurring Financial Detriment Arising From The Loss Of Data.

Proponents of cryptocurrency in its early stages contended that, given adequate safeguards, alternative digital currencies have the capacity to facilitate a substantial transition away from conventional cash, which they perceived as flawed and potentially hazardous. It is advisable to store one's funds in a cloud-based system or a physical data storage device, rather than carrying them in a personal pocket or handbag, given the presence of highly secure source code, robust authentication protocols, and effective safeguards against hacking.

This, nevertheless, presupposes that cryptocurrency users undertake the requisite measures to avert data loss. In the event that a user's private keys are confined to a solitary physical storage medium, such as a device that is subsequently misplaced or pilfered, the user will endure irreversible financial repercussions. Furthermore, users who exclusively rely on a single cloud service face the potential jeopardy of data loss in the event of severe physical damage to the server or disconnection from the Internet, particularly if the server is operated in a jurisdiction with stringent Internet regulations, such as China.

Significant Price Fluctuations and Susceptibility to Manipulation

A significant portion of cryptocurrencies exhibit a limited supply, with a concentration of ownership primarily among a select group of individuals, often including the currency's creators and closely affiliated parties. Similar to thinly traded penny stocks, these holders effectively oversee the supply of these currencies, making them susceptible to unpredictable price swings and potential exploitation. Nevertheless, frequently traded cryptocurrencies are susceptible to market volatility, as demonstrated by Bitcoin's value experiencing multiple instances of doubling in 2017, followed by a significant decrease in the initial weeks of 2018.

Perpetually non-convertible to fiat currency.

Only the cryptocurrencies that are most frequently traded, featuring the highest market capitalization in terms of USD, possess specialized online platforms enabling direct conversion into fiat currencies. The remaining options lack specialized online platforms, thus rendering them unable to be directly exchanged for fiat currencies. Alternatively, users are required to first convert them into widely-accepted cryptocurrencies, such as Bitcoin, prior to converting them into fiat currency. Through the increase in transaction costs, the demand and subsequent value of less commonly utilized cryptocurrencies are diminished.

Chargebacks and refunds may be subject to restrictions or may not be available.

Despite cryptocurrency miners acting as quasi-intermediaries in cryptocurrency transactions, they lack the capability to address disputes between the parties involved. In actuality, the concept of a decentralized arbitrator is in opposition to the central tenet of decentralization that lies at the heart of contemporary cryptocurrency ideology. This means you have no one to turn to if you're duped in a cryptocurrency deal, such as paying in advance for something you never get. Although certain emerging cryptocurrencies attempt to address the challenge of chargebacks and refunds, the proposed solutions are still in their nascent phases and have yet to be thoroughly tested and validated.

In contrast, conventional payment service providers and established credit card networks such as Visa, MasterCard, and PayPal frequently intercede in disputes between buyers and sellers. Their restitution strategies, commonly referred to as chargeback protocols, aim to discourage instances of seller deception.

The Detrimental Ecological Consequences of Cryptocurrency Mining

Cryptocurrency mining necessitates substantial resource consumption. Bitcoin, the globally renowned digital currency, stands as the primary candidate under scrutiny. According to data mentioned by Ars Technica, the energy consumption of Bitcoin mining exceeds that of the entire nation of Denmark. However, unlike the comparatively minimal carbon footprint of the equitable Scandinavian state, certain significant Bitcoin mining operations are situated in countries abundant in coal resources, such as China.

Cryptocurrency experts concur that mining presents a considerable ecological risk given the current pace of development, albeit they are expeditious in discarding the most sensationalistic contentions. As reported by Ars Technica, three prospective short- to medium-term remedies have been identified.

• Reducing the value of Bitcoin with the aim of diminishing the profitability of mining, a step that would likely entail coordinated intervention in a market that has hitherto operated freely.

• Accelerating the decrease in the mining incentive beyond the originally planned rate of halving every four years.

• Adopting a more energy-efficient algorithm, which is a subject of debate within the mining industry.

In the long run, the most effective approach entails powering cryptocurrency mines using low- or zero-emission energy sources, and potentially incentivizing the relocation of these mines to countries with low carbon footprints, like Costa Rica and the Netherlands.

EXAMPLES OF CRYPTOCURRENCY

Ever since Bitcoin was introduced, the utilization of digital currencies has experienced a dramatic surge. Despite the ever-changing active currency figures and the highly volatile nature of individual currency values, the collective market capitalization of all active cryptocurrencies is demonstrating a consistent upward trajectory. Numerous digital currencies are actively exchanged at any given moment.

The subsequent digital currencies exhibit a consistent level of acceptance, substantial user engagement, and a comparatively substantial market capitalization (in many instances, exceeding $10 million, though valuations are subject to fluctuations):

1. Bitcoin

Bitcoin is widely regarded as the preeminent cryptocurrency on a global scale, playing a pivotal role in integrating the phenomenon of digital currencies into mainstream financial landscapes. The cryptocurrency in question consistently boasts a market capitalization and unit value that surpass those of the second most prevalent digital currency by a significant margin, often exceeding it by a factor of 10 or more. The quantity of Bitcoin in circulation is capped at a maximum of 21 million units.

Bitcoin is gaining increased recognition and legitimacy as a permissible means of financial transaction. Numerous renowned enterprises have adopted the practice of accepting payments made in Bitcoin. Nevertheless, the majority of individuals opt to utilize a cryptocurrency exchange platform to convert Bitcoin into U.S. dollars prior to acquiring funds.

2. Litecoin

Litecoin, introduced in 2011, exhibits analogous fundamental characteristics to Bitcoin. Two primary distinctions can be observed. Firstly, there is an elevated programmed limit on the supply, reaching 84 million units. Secondly, there is a notable reduction in the time required for blockchain construction, at only two-and-a-half minutes. The encryption algorithm exhibits certain variations as well. In terms of its market capitalization, Litecoin often ranks as the second or third most prevalent cryptocurrency.

3. Ripple

Ripple, having been introduced in 2012, is widely recognized for its utilization of "consensus ledger" technology, resulting in substantially decreased transaction confirmation periods and accelerated blockchain establishment. There is no specific predetermined time frame; however, the typical interval is every few seconds. Ripple can also be exchanged expeditiously compared to other cryptocurrencies, courtesy of an internal currency exchange mechanism, which facilitates the conversion of Ripple units into prominent currencies such as U.S. dollars, yen, euros, and others.

Furthermore, adversaries have also raised concerns regarding the susceptibility of Ripple's network and code to sophisticated hackers, as well as the diminished level of confidentiality inherent in such cryptocurrencies derived from Bitcoin.

4. Ethereum

Ethereum, introduced in the year 2015, enhances the fundamental framework of Bitcoin through various improvements. Intelligent agreements, more specifically, are utilized for the purpose of ensuring the fulfillment of a transaction, compelling involved parties to uphold their commitments, and offering provisions for restitution in case of contract breach. Although "smart contracts" represent a notable advancement in addressing the absence of chargebacks and refunds in cryptocurrencies, it remains uncertain whether they will prove sufficient in completely resolving this issue.

5. Dogecoin

Dogecoin can be characterized as a derivative of Litecoin, which stands out due to its readily recognizable mascot, the Shiba Inu. It exhibits significantly accelerated blockchain generation time (approximately one minute) and a substantially greater quantity of coins in circulation. The founders successfully achieved their objective of mining 100 billion units by July 2015, and subsequently implemented a yearly mining limit of 5.2 billion units, imposing no predetermined supply constraint. Consequently, Dogecoin stands out as a noteworthy experiment in the realm of "inflationary cryptocurrency," which prompts analysts to closely monitor its long-term value trajectory in relation to other cryptocurrencies.

6. Coinye

Coinye, a cryptocurrency that is no longer in operation, garners attention solely due to its peculiar background.

Coinye was established in 2013 under the appellation "Coinye West" and is characterized by an evident semblance to the celebrated hip-hop luminary, Kanye West. In the beginning of 2014, just prior to the anticipated release of Coinye, the legal representatives of Mr. West became aware of the existence of the cryptocurrency and issued a formal notification demanding the immediate cessation of its production by the creators.

In order to mitigate potential legal consequences, the developers opted to remove the term "West" from the name, substituted the logo with a depiction of a "half man, half fish hybrid" resembling West (in a satirical nod to a "South Park" episode that ridiculed West's immense ego), and proceeded with the anticipated release of Coinye. The currency garnered a fervent following among enthusiasts of cryptocurrencies owing to the exhilaration and ironic wit encompassing its launch. Notwithstanding this, West's legal team initiated legal proceedings, demanding that the founders divest their shares and cease operations of the Coinye website.

Despite the fact that the peer-to-peer network of Coinye is presently functioning, and mining the currency remains a theoretical possibility, the value of the currency has dramatically declined to such an extent that it is essentially devoid of practical worth.

Cryptocurrency is an intriguing concept that possesses the capacity to revolutionize the landscape of worldwide financial systems in a positive manner. Despite being founded on solid, egalitarian ideals, cryptocurrency remains a field that requires technical expertise and practical application. It is highly likely that national governments will continue to hold a dominant position in the production of currency and formulation of monetary policies in the foreseeable future.

In the meantime, individuals who engage in cryptocurrency transactions (as well as those who are captivated by the potential of this concept) need to maintain a perpetual awareness regarding the pragmatic constraints associated with it. Caution should be exercised in regard to suggestions promoting the notion that a particular cryptocurrency ensures absolute anonymity or shields from legal responsibility, as well as assertions highlighting individual cryptocurrencies as infallible investment prospects or safeguards against inflation. While gold is often acclaimed as the ultimate safeguard against inflation, it is nonetheless susceptible to profound uncertainty, possibly to a greater extent than several prominent fiat currencies in developed economies.

Is the Implementation of Proof of Stake Likely to Eliminate Ethereum Mining?

The proposed concept of Ethereum 2.0 seeks to implement a transition to proof-of-Stake, a consensus algorithm that aims to provide current Ethereum network miners with a limited opportunity to obtain a return on their investment.

• It is customary to be dispatched at the conclusion of 2021 or the commencement of 2022. It is imperative that it be dispatched no later than October 2020; however, it is worth delving into the history of delays surrounding this upgrade.

• The precise timeline for the completion and integration of Ethereum 2.0 into the Cryptocurrency mining ecosystem remains uncertain to all.

In this vein, it is anticipated that Proof of Work mining will remain viable until 2022.

proof of-Stake

Is Mining Ethereum Productive?

• The profitability of cryptocurrency mining is heavily contingent on the cost of electricity in the given area.

In a broad sense, any amount less than $0.12 per kilowatt-hour is regarded as advantageous.

• By analyzing metrics such as the Ethereum hash rate, block reward, and block count, you have the opportunity to engage in Ether mining and convert it into a vital source of income. per day, along with the Ethereum coin's associated expenditure.

• You have the option to employ an Ethereum computational tool in order to organize your daily earnings, basing the calculations on these factors.

Ethereum Mini-computer

• Alternatively, you can also utilize this formula.

The daily income can be calculated as follows: multiply your hash rate by the block reward, multiply this result by the number of blocks in a day, and then multiply this by the current value of the coin. Finally, divide this figure by the overall hash rate.

It is anticipated that the price of ETH may increase and exhibit greater stability in the foreseeable future. In accordance with this reasoning, it presents an excellent opportunity to invest in and preserve funds in Ethereum.

The History Of Nft

Cryptocurrency revolves around the principle of decentralization. It is a form of technology that is gradually integrating into our everyday experiences. May I inquire about the nature and characteristics of decentralized technology? The response to that inquiry encompasses intricate aspects. However, we may consider it as a decentralized entity without any central authority or governing body. To put it differently, it pertains to a form of technology that is possessed collectively by individuals, as opposed to being under the ownership of any particular corporation or entity.

Taking into consideration the aforementioned, it becomes apparent how the notion of non-fungible tokens (NFTs) aligns logically within the domain of cryptocurrency. If you are a novice in the realm of cryptocurrencies, you might be unfamiliar with the concept of Non-Fungible Tokens (NFTs).

Let us now delve into the historical origins of NFTs and examine their progression.

Could you kindly provide information regarding the initial emergence and temporal context of NFTs?

We have deliberated upon the causal relationship between Bitcoin and the subsequent emergence and proliferation of cryptocurrencies. However, there existed a predecessor in the realm of technology that laid the groundwork for Bitcoin's emergence.

It's called a blockchain. The existence of cryptocurrency is made possible thanks to the implementation of blockchain technology. In the absence of a blockchain, the transmission and reception of monetary transactions would be unfeasible across the internet.

Presently, it is evident that non-fungible tokens (NFTs) have experienced significant surge in popularity in recent years, thus establishing their prominence in the forthcoming era of cryptocurrency. However, from whence did they originate? The genesis of this endeavor can be traced back to the conceptualization of an individual by the name of Nick Szabo.

Nick Szabo is an individual hailing from the United States who possesses expertise in the realms of computer science and cryptography. He is widely acknowledged as the pioneer behind the development of the inaugural smart contract. This contractual agreement was devised upon a game titled "The Fermi Paradox," which he ingeniously formulated in the year 1995.

In this gaming scenario, participants would engage in the direct transfer of a digital asset to another participant, without utilizing intermediary entities such as banks or PayPal. In order to accomplish this, it would be necessary to transmit the digital asset to an undisclosed public key address, and subsequently rely on the chance of it reaching the intended recipient. If the funds did not reach their intended destination, then the possibility of permanently forfeiting your money would have ensued, unless an intermediary facilitated its transmission on your behalf.

Contemporary Non-Fungible Tokens

Taking this into consideration, it becomes apparent that Nick Szabo had conceived the concept of non-fungible tokens (NFTs) well in advance, predating the emergence of cryptocurrencies. In the contemporary era, a wide array of diverse NFTs find application across a multitude of industries and global undertakings. Prominent entities in the world of NFTs encompass CryptoKitties, Etheremon, and CryptoPunks.

These aforementioned projects have significantly impacted the realm of NFTs. Countless others with similar merits can be discovered on platforms such as Enjin. Enjin is a specialized platform designed for the purpose of creating and facilitating the exchange of NFTs. It functions as an electronic marketplace, enabling users to engage in the buying and selling of diverse digital assets.

It is imperative to bear in mind that these digital assets do not pertain to physical entities, as they are rooted in blockchain technology and thus inaccessible to tactile or visual perception. Nevertheless, certain non-fungible tokens (NFTs) also possess tangible manifestations, exemplified by entities like CryptoPunks and GigaPets offered by Rare Bits.

Etheremon is a renowned NFT initiative that leverages blockchain technology to generate virtual creatures grounded on the Ethereum blockchain. These creatures possess utility in confrontations and exhibit absolute distinctiveness, rendering them irretrievable subsequent to their sale or trade.

The prevalence of NFTs is increasingly gaining momentum with each passing day, indicating their enduring presence in the market. Numerous companies are entering the domain by initiating their own NFT initiatives. However, it is crucial to bear in mind that these initiatives can present significant perplexity and potential hazard to investors lacking comprehension of the operational intricacies of blockchain technology.

CryptoKitties

CryptoKitties is an interactive digital game operating on a blockchain platform, which facilitates the virtual acquisition, trade, and reproduction of feline avatars. It was developed by Axiom Zen, a Vancouver-based Canadian company. The game attained widespread popularity following the launch of CryptoKitties in November 2017.

CryptoKitties serves as a compelling illustration of how Non-Fungible Tokens (NFTs) can be harnessed to develop decentralized applications (DApps). It stands as a pioneering game that implements blockchain technology and exemplifies its potential in crafting an entertaining experience for the general populace.

The primary objective of CryptoKitties is to engage in the breeding of exclusive feline specimens that possess significant value within the marketplace. You commence with a pair of felines, which can subsequently be mated in the aspiration of procuring uncommon progeny.

There are numerous factors that contribute to the excellence of CryptoKitties as a game. One primary aspect to consider is the inherent enjoyment derived from engaging in the activity. It is an engaging interactive game that facilitates the creation of novel virtual felines endowed with distinctive characteristics and attributes. This elevates it beyond a mere game. It serves as a means for artistic expression, while also presenting lucrative investment prospects.

If you're new to the crypto space, you may be wondering how exactly CryptoKitties work.

How Does CryptoKitties Work?

CryptoKitties operates by leveraging smart contracts deployed on the Ethereum blockchain. This means that the Kitties are owned by their owners and not by anyone else. On the marketplace, one has the freedom to purchase, vend, or engage in the reproduction of felines without interference or obstruction. Every transaction is meticulously documented on the blockchain, without any centralized entity overseeing them.

Furthermore, each Kitty possesses a distinct set of individual characteristics or traits. These distinguishing characteristics encompass attributes such as hue, design, ocular pigmentation, and pelage pattern, all of which are arbitrarily generated upon the inception of a novel feline entity on the blockchain infrastructure. These characteristics may be inherited by offspring through the process of breeding, leading to the emergence of novel traits and combinations.

All of these characteristics and their corresponding values are securely stored and documented on the blockchain. This implies that they are beyond alteration or modification in any manner. Due to the fact that the kittens are legally possessed by their respective owners, there lacks a centralized governing body with the capacity to exercise the authority to separate them from their owners.

What is the method of purchasing CryptoKitties?

If you desire to acquire a CryptoKitty, the initial step entails establishing an account on the respective platform. After completing this step, you will be able to proceed to the marketplace where you can acquire a Kitty from one of the vendors available. Subsequently, a private key will be provided to you, granting access to your Kitty via the blockchain.

This specific private key is exclusive to your individual account and exclusively functions with your unique Kitty. Therefore, in the event that an unauthorized individual obtains access to it, they will be unable to retrieve your Kitty, even if they possess an exact replica of their own. Consequently, the sole means by which anyone other than yourself could obtain possession of your Kitty is with your explicit consent.

What is the valuation of CryptoKitties?

When CryptoKitties initially debuted, their value was comparatively modest in relation to their current worth. Initially, the CryptoKitties possessed a modest value of approximately $10 apiece, rendering them attainable for a wide range of individuals. However, owing to the surging participation in CryptoKitties, their worth has experienced a substantial escalation.

Currently, the value of an individual CryptoKitty can range from $100 to $20,000. And as the number of individuals expressing interest in these items continues to grow daily, their worth is poised to escalate in the forthcoming times. Therefore, if you are considering participating in CryptoKitties, the present moment presents an opportune occasion to commence your engagement.

Are CryptoKitties Legal?

Indeed, possessing a CryptoKitty is fully permissible under the law, and they are entirely compliant with the blockchain platform on which they operate. The United States Securities and Exchange

Commission (SEC) has characterized them as a type of investment asset, thereby establishing the requirement that purchasers must be no younger than 18 years of age. Consequently, purchasing a CryptoKitty is in violation of the law for individuals under the age of 18. Moreover, it is unlawful for individuals without possession of their own private key, as well as the associated Kitty, to engage in the acquisition of these feline characters. Therefore, if you are contemplating purchasing a Kitty as a present for someone, it is imperative to verify that the recipient is of legal age, namely 18 years or older, prior to engaging in such a transaction.

Crypto Art

Cryptocurrency revolves around the concept of decentralization. It is a technological innovation that is gradually becoming an integrated part of our everyday routines. And could you please elaborate on the concept of decentralized technology? The response to that inquiry can be rather intricate.

However, we can examine it as an entity devoid of any central authority or governing body. Stated differently, it can be inferred that this technology is collectively owned by the individuals rather than being under the ownership of a specific corporation or institution.

Considering this perspective, it becomes apparent how the notion of non-fungible tokens aligns harmoniously with the domain of cryptocurrency. If you possess limited knowledge of the cryptocurrency realm, you might be unfamiliar with the concept of non-fungible tokens (NFTs).

What is Crypto art?

To put it succinctly, Crypto Art represents the unification of the blockchain sphere and the realm of art. From a more technical perspective, it can be defined as a distinctive digital asset that possesses the capability to be traded on different cryptocurrency exchanges.

The initial instance of crypto art can be identified as CryptoKitties. These virtual felines are available for purchase and trade, with a finite quantity available.

Nonetheless, there exist no defined criteria that govern the formation of these felines. Each specimen is distinct, and it is possible for it to be possessed by an individual or a collective entity.

These digital assets bear resemblance to stocks in terms of ownership and value, yet they possess a distinctive attribute in that their quantity and creation process is unregulated by any predetermined algorithm. These feline entities are not subject to any centralized rules, regulations, or governing bodies pertaining to their creation.

In the present day, a multitude of digital artists spanning the globe are engrossed in the creation of distinctive crypto art. In the coming years, this sector is expected to hold great promise as one of the most captivating industries within the realm of blockchain technology. There exist numerous platforms, including OpenSea and RareBits, which enable individuals to engage in the purchasing and selling of digital art.

What is the process for conducting transactions involving NFTs?

Crypto art is at an early stage of development, however, there are avenues available for its buying and selling. A significant number of individuals opt for decentralized exchanges as a means to engage in the trading of digital artwork. These exchanges function in a comparable manner to stock exchanges, albeit distinguished by a highly distinctive and adaptable framework.

Additionally, a considerable number of individuals employ crypto art as a means of capitalizing on their investments. They perceive it as a means of generating revenue, but they also view it as a prospect to lend assistance to artists globally. These artists are producing exquisite pieces of artwork that are traded on a daily basis. Certain artwork within the realm of cryptocurrency has even garnered multi-million dollar valuations! These developments in the field of crypto art are indeed thrilling, and we can anticipate further progress and success within this vibrant industry moving forward.

Chapter Three: Cryptocurrency Trading and Investment

To engage in the investment and trading of cryptocurrencies, it is essential to familiarize oneself with the principles of acquiring and securely storing these digital assets. The majority of cryptocurrencies follow a standard protocol for storage, purchase, and trading. Therefore, we shall employ Bitcoin as an illustrative example to elucidate the process.

Step 1: Acquiring

The primary method to obtain Bitcoins is by engaging in computer mining, which has gained significant popularity among individuals. Although this method may not be the most cost-effective or straightforward, it does yield the attainment of free Bitcoin through your mining endeavors. It constitutes a set of intricate mathematical equations that are resolved through computational means. This delineates the original process by which Bitcoins were forged and the ongoing mechanism through which additional units are introduced into circulation. At the point of this publication, an estimated quantity of 25 Bitcoins are generated every 10 minutes through the utilization of these intricate computational systems and their mathematical algorithms.

An alternative method that is considerably more convenient would be to locate a reputable Bitcoin exchange and proceed with the straightforward acquisition of Bitcoins. Given the prevalence of these exchanges and the inherent nature of the currency, it is imperative that you exercise careful consideration and choose an exchange that guarantees protection from fraudulent activities. Refrain from engaging with any company or person purporting to assist with Bitcoin mining, any offers that appear excessively attractive but suspicious, or anything that evokes a generally negative perception. In an ideal situation, you should possess the capacity to conduct thorough research on the specific Bitcoin exchange and promptly access substantial amounts of relevant information pertaining to it. Please ensure that you consistently conduct thorough research on the exchange to safeguard against any potential fraudulent practices. Given the current elevated worth of Bitcoin, there has been an upsurge in fraudulent activities where individuals seek to deceive others and unlawfully seize their financial resources. It is imperative that you exercise caution and take measures to safeguard yourself against becoming a target of these deceitful actions. Another noteworthy element to consider is the presence of pyramid schemes that are associated with Bitcoin. Although these options may seem lucrative or appear to offer investment assistance, they will not yield financial savings, and ultimately, you may find yourself without any Bitcoin.

Notwithstanding the prevalence of various scams associated with Bitcoin, it is crucial for one to comprehend that it is not justifiable to entirely forsake the Bitcoin currency on these grounds. It is important to note that conventional currencies, despite the possibility of fraudulent activities, retain significant worth and play an indispensable role in our society's day-to-day functioning. Bitcoins do not possess indispensable utility in our everyday existence, however, they retain significant worth and offer substantial potential for profit and prosperity to individuals who acquire or invest in them.

It is essential to prioritize the utilization of reputable and authenticated sources when procuring your Bitcoin. After the identification of a suitable cryptocurrency exchange, you are able to commence trading Bitcoin without any restrictions, engaging in investments according to your preference. This method offers a straightforward and secure approach to participate in Bitcoin ownership and trading, while mitigating concerns of potential fraudulent activities or financial exploitation within the realm of cryptocurrencies.

Cryptocurrency Exchanges

A cryptocurrency exchange refers to a virtual platform that enables the acquisition, sale, and swapping of cryptocurrencies with other digital currencies or traditional fiat currencies such as US dollars and British pounds. There exist various forms of cryptocurrency exchanges, each catering to distinct individuals based on their specific requirements.

If your objective is to engage in professional trading and utilize sophisticated trading tools, there exist advanced exchanges that cater to such requirements. The majority of these will require authentication of your identity prior to establishing a trading account. For individuals seeking a singular or sporadic trading opportunity, there exist convenient platforms that facilitate trade transactions without necessitating the establishment of a dedicated trading account.

There exist three distinct classifications of cryptocurrency exchanges:

• Trading platforms: These platforms serve as intermediaries between traders and facilitate transactions, for which they levy a fee on each transaction conducted. They fulfill the function of serving as an intermediary, responsible for safeguarding both cryptocurrencies and fiat money, as well as managing the execution of transactions and exchanges.

• Platforms for direct trading: These are also commonly referred to as peer-to-peer markets. In contrast to trading platforms that function as intermediaries, direct trading platforms facilitate direct exchange between buyers and sellers. Direct trading platforms do not possess a predetermined market price. The determination of exchange rates lies within the purview of sellers.

• Brokers and direct commercial exchanges: These Internet platforms operate in a manner akin to that of foreign exchange brokers. They permit individuals to readily purchase cryptocurrencies at predetermined prices established by the exchange.

Picking an Exchange

There exist a multitude of cryptocurrency exchanges accessible to individuals seeking to engage in cryptocurrency trading. Nevertheless, it would be inadvisable to participate in an exchange merely by chance, without taking other factors into consideration. Prior to enrolling in an exchange program, it is advised to take into account the following variables.

Esteem: The primary step to undertake when contemplating a particular exchange is to carefully peruse testimonials from other users who have availed themselves of the exchange, in addition to consulting official platforms within the industry. Explore digital platforms and online forums where individuals with a penchant for cryptocurrencies congregate, and graciously pose any inquiries or concerns you may hold regarding a particular exchange.

Fees: Users of cryptocurrency exchanges are levied with transaction, deposit, and withdrawal fees. This is the factor that sustains their operations. Various exchanges possess distinct fee structures. The majority of typical exchanges implement a fee structure based on trading volume, which enables individuals engaged in substantial trades to benefit from reduced fees. Prior to enrolling in an exchange, ensure that you possess comprehensive knowledge regarding their fee framework. The majority of this information can readily be accessed on the website of the exchange.

Accepted forms of payment: Prior to enrolling in an exchange, ascertain the range of payment methods that are supported and evaluate their suitability based on your preferences. Please kindly note that utilizing credit cards and PayPal will incur additional fees, whereas the processing time for receiving your cryptocurrency may be extended if opting for bank transfers.

Identity verification is typically mandatory for individuals seeking to deposit or withdraw funds on the majority of cryptocurrency exchanges in the United States and United Kingdom, whereas certain platforms offer the option of maintaining complete anonymity. Despite appearing contrary to the ethos of cryptocurrencies, the process of verification serves to safeguard the exchange from instances of money laundering and fraudulent activities.

Geographical limitations: Certain exchanges may possess features that can solely be accessed within designated geographical areas or nations. Prior to enrolling in an exchange program, it is imperative to ascertain that it proffers comprehensive assistance within your jurisdiction.

Currency exchange rates: Varying rates of exchange exist across different cryptocurrency trading platforms. Examine various exchanges in order to ascertain the one that presents the most favorable price for the cryptocurrency in which you plan to engage in trading.

Different Exchanges

Outlined below are the top five cryptocurrency exchanges, which have been determined based on a comprehensive evaluation of various criteria, encompassing user feedback, security measures, fee framework, accessibility, and ease of use.

Coinbase

This particular cryptocurrency exchange is widely recognized as one of the most renowned and highly frequented platforms globally. Commenced in the year of 2012, it possesses a commendable standing, an authoritative support from reputable investors, and a substantial user base in the millions. The Coinbase platform exemplifies a high degree of user-friendliness and convenience, granting users the capacity to securely execute purchases, sales, storage, and transactions involving cryptocurrencies. Coinbase provides support for the digital currencies Bitcoin, Ether, and Litecoin. Additionally, it offers a mobile wallet that is accessible on both Android and iOS platforms. Customers have the opportunity to acquire cryptocurrency via a mobile wallet or engage in trading activities with fellow users on the Global Digital Asset Exchange (GDAX), a subsidiary establishment of Coinbase. Coinbase is widely recognized for its robust security measures, competitive fee structure, and intuitive user interface. The funds held within Coinbase are additionally protected under the coverage of Coinbase insurance. Nevertheless, Coinbase displays restrained support for various countries, offers a limited array of payment options, and its GDAX platform caters more specifically to proficient users.

Kraken

This establishment is an exchange located in San Francisco, having been established in the year 2011. Kraken and Fidor have joined forces to develop the pioneering concept of the world's inaugural digital currency bank. Furthermore, it is worth noting that it is equipped with seamless integration capabilities with Bloomberg terminals.

Kraken affords users the opportunity to engage in trading of Bitcoin and a diverse range of international currencies, encompassing U.S. dollars, Canadian dollars, British pounds, euros, and Japanese yen. In addition, Kraken offers support for a diverse range of alternative digital currencies such as Bitcoin, Ethereum, Ethereum Classic, Ripple, Dogecoin, Monero, Litecoin, Stellar, Zcash, and ICONOMI. Kraken is widely renowned for its exceptional reputation, competitive deposit and transaction fees, favorable exchange rates, extensive range of features, global support network, and exemplary user assistance services. The limitations of this product can be attributed to the restricted range of payment methods available and a user interface that lacks intuitiveness, making it less user-friendly for inexperienced individuals.

Poloniex

Established in 2014, Poloniex has emerged as one of the leading global cryptocurrency exchanges, renowned for its substantial trade volume. It facilitates the conversion of Bitcoin into over 100 varieties of alternative cryptocurrencies. Registering for an account on Poloniex is expedient and effortless. The platform provides a comprehensive and intuitive interface, equipped with sophisticated analysis tools tailored for proficient users. Poloniex boasts one of the most competitive fee structures in the realm of cryptocurrency exchanges. The quality of user support is commendable, as it provides a chat interface enabling users to seek assistance from fellow users. The moderators maintain the integrity of the chat box by removing any comments that are deemed inappropriate. In addition, Poloniex provides BTC lending services and maintains an accessible API. One drawback of Poloniex is its lack of support for fiat currencies.

Shapeshift

Established in the year 2013, Shapeshift is a prompt cryptocurrency exchange platform enabling users to interchange different types of cryptocurrencies. Shapeshift offers its endorsement to Bitcoin along with various alternative cryptocurrencies such as Ethereum, Dash, Dogecoin, Monero, and Zcash. Regrettably, Shapeshift does not facilitate conversions between digital currencies and traditional fiat currencies. One of the primary benefits of Shapeshift is that it facilitates the exchange of cryptocurrencies while ensuring a paramount degree of anonymity for individuals. Customers have the ability to engage in cryptocurrency exchanges without the necessity of establishing an account. It does not store funds within a centralized exchange. Shapeshift garners a favorable standing, boasting a user interface conducive to novices, conveyance of reasonable pricing, and a wide-ranging support for myriad cryptocurrencies.

LocalBitcoins

This platform serves as a well-known peer-to-peer marketplace facilitating connections between Bitcoin sellers and buyers residing in the same city or geographic area. It extends its support to numerous cities across the globe. Through LocalBitcoins, traders have the flexibility to determine their preferred payment method or arrange for in-person meetups to facilitate the transaction. The platform affords sellers the ability to establish their own exchange rates, while concurrently imposing a commission of 1 percent on each transaction. In order to uphold the platform's security, it employs a reputation ranking system and maintains a publicly accessible record of every user's transactions. Additionally, it possesses an escrow service that acts as a custodian for funds, solely disbursing them once the seller confirms the completion of the trade. Registration on LocalBitcoins does not mandate the verification of personal identification. It offers a complimentary, user-friendly means of acquiring Bitcoins, facilitates transactions in diverse local currencies based on geographical location, and is accessible across the globe. One disadvantage of this option is the relatively elevated exchange rates it offers, making it a less favorable choice for purchasing substantial quantities of Bitcoin.

Step 2: Storing

Similar to conventional currency, Bitcoins possess a digital "wallet" that serves as a repository for their storage.

This wallet is generated automatically upon the initial purchase of your first Bitcoin, and it is subsequently maintained for your exclusive use. When you procure Bitcoin or allocate an investment towards this particular cryptocurrency, it will be enlisted in your digital wallet. In like manner, each instance of currency expenditure will result in a deduction from this digital wallet.

Your digital wallet can be found either directly on your computer or within the cloud storage system. This wallet functions similarly to a bank, meticulously recording the inflow and outflow of Bitcoin to and from your wallet. This wallet offers versatile functionalities, allowing you to facilitate transactions, manage funds, and securely store your Bitcoin assets.

It is essential to comprehend, nonetheless, that there are potential hazards associated with your digital wallet that possess irreversible consequences, if they were to occur. For instance, as the wallet lacks insurance coverage from the FDIC, it is imperative to note that any discrepancies or loss of funds cannot be recovered or restored through insurance facilities. Additionally, it is important to consider certain aspects concerning the storage location of the wallet. For wallets that are stored in the cloud, some companies may have the power to take more Bitcoin than you have approved or otherwise take your currency. Moreover, it is worth noting that servers possess vulnerability to unauthorized access, thereby creating an avenue for hackers to potentially compromise the security of your Bitcoin and pilfer it for personal gain. In the event that you choose to keep your wallet stored on your computer, there is a susceptibility to hacking, virus-induced damage, potential deletion, or loss in the unfortunate circumstances of a computer malfunction.

Step 3: Trading

In the forthcoming year of 2018, Nasdaq will initiate the trading of Bitcoin, heralding a new phase in the proliferation of digital currency. Trading will be especially profitable for individuals who demonstrated their willingness to persevere amidst the volatile fluctuations in the value of the coins. The standard practice entails purchasing when the price declines and disposing of assets when the price rises. Due to the significant volatility in the values over the course of a day, traders have the potential to engage in numerous transactions within a single 24-hour timeframe. Numerous individuals have consistently accumulated substantial amounts of wealth.

To commence your trading journey, it is imperative that you make a prudent decision regarding the cryptocurrency assets you intend to utilize. Certain traders exclusively utilize a singular cryptocurrency as a foundation for their trades, relying solely on its fluctuations in value. Some individuals engage in cryptocurrency trading to leverage trends spanning the entirety of the crypto-economy. Additionally, it will be necessary to procure a suitable trading platform and deliberate upon the specific strategies you wish to employ. Commencing your trading journey by collaborating with a seasoned trader until you acquire proficiency can serve as an invaluable means to acquire optimal trading methodologies.

Stage 4: Generating Revenue

Making money with cryptocurrencies is not particularly difficult, and in this section, we will look at the different ways in which you can do this.

We are open to receiving payment in digital currencies.

If you possess the capability to accept funds from individuals, it is within your purview to solicit cryptocurrency payments. If you possess an internet-based enterprise or a physical retail establishment, you have the capacity to facilitate transactions through cryptocurrencies. There exist applications that can be employed to facilitate their utilization. You may discover an increased proclivity among individuals to endorse your business solely due to your accommodation of their preferred payment methods. Perhaps your acquaintances or relatives could be willing to provide you with financial assistance. It is possible to make a formal request for them to facilitate the transmission of the payment to you in digital currency. Simply provide them with the address associated with your account.

Mining

Mining is the procedure through which fresh cryptocurrency tokens are generated. When a cluster of transactions is consolidated into a block, it is necessary to unravel a sophisticated mathematical puzzle in order to authenticate the transactions. Miners employ their computer systems to resolve these enigmas. Subsequently, fresh tokens are generated, with a customary allocation given as a reward to the miner who successfully resolved the puzzle.

In order to commence mining, it is essential to possess a robust computer, employ specialized hardware and software, and access affordable energy resources. You seek affordable energy due to the substantial energy requirements of mining, which can result in rapid loss of profitability. Maintaining a consistent access to wind, solar, or alternative renewable sources of energy will aid in safeguarding the preservation of your financial gains by preventing energy expenses from nullifying their worth.

Prior to initiating the mining process, it is imperative that you conduct a thorough assessment of the specific cryptocurrency you intend to mine. Mining Bitcoins is no longer profitable for individuals because the hardware has advanced so much that it is incredibly expensive. The majority of Bitcoin mining takes place at establishments commonly referred to as "mining farms." Alternative cryptocurrencies, such as LSK and Dash, employ distinct mining protocols that restrict mining activities to specific individuals. In order to engage in LSK mining, it is necessary to hold a distinguished position within the community and obtain a nomination. Dash has classified the mining process into two distinct categories, comprising of the "mining elite" and the "common" miners. This aims to guarantee the swift transaction time that Dash pledges.

There exist alternative cryptocurrencies, such as Dogecoin and Ether, which can be readily mined by individuals. Given that Dogecoin does not yield significant profitability and is regarded as a community centered around amusement and casualness, there exists little motivation to develop hardware with progressively enhanced capabilities. Consequently, minimal investment is needed apart from possessing a reliable Internet connection, a computer with ample storage capacity, and access to affordable energy. Ether can be extracted by any individual. With the substantial profitability it has garnered, companies are driven to develop increasingly robust hardware for the purpose of mining it. Consequently, the process of mining Ether may escalate in cost over time.

One possible alternative to engaging in individual mining with your personal computer is to partake in a mining consortium or network, commonly referred to as a mining pool. A mining pool refers to a collective arrangement wherein individuals amalgamate their computational resources to enhance the speed at which they can solve block hashes, thereby increasing their likelihood of obtaining rewards. The accolades are subsequently divided amongst the various constituents of the mining consortium, in proportion to the extent of their computational prowess.

What Is The Definition Of Nodes And Master-Nodes?

The node functions as a wallet that has not achieved complete synchronization (exceeding 100 GB) with the blockchain network.

Full Nodes, which also function as complete network nodes, maintain constant synchronization with the blockchain of connected wallets throughout the entire duration of 24/7 network connectivity. The purpose of their role is to serve as repositories of comprehensive network information, performing the essential task of scrutinizing new transactions for their compliance with the network's established regulations, subsequently approving or disapproving their inclusion within newly created blocks. Loyal nods are performed by the enthusiastic patrons of the establishment without any form of remuneration.

Miners are electronic systems that generate fresh blockchain blocks within the network by processing bitcoins, along with validating new transactions as approved by the nodes.

Master-nodes are comprehensively synchronized wallets that maintain a continuous connection to the network throughout the entirety of every day. Their primary purpose is to support the network, encompassing various activities spanning from executing transactions to offering supplementary features, such as ensuring absolute transaction confidentiality (for instance, in Dash, transactions are not recorded in the blockchain), and other similar functionalities. based on the technological characteristics of individual master codes

Given that master nodes are to some extent involved in the processing of transactions, they receive a portion of the newly discovered coins in a fresh block, thereby sharing the profits with the miners.

Is it advisable for me to immobilize my funds by investing in a masterpiece?

While it is true that the risk ratio of the deposit amount in the master course and the monthly profit is typically considerable, it is noteworthy that the prospects for the exponential growth of coins enabled by this technology are rather appealing.

8. Cryptocurrency storage

Individuals who have made the resolution to convert their savings into a cryptocurrency or participate in cryptocurrency earnings find themselves promptly pondering the matter of cryptocurrency storage and the selection of a dependable wallet.

The absence of such storage renders the accumulation or utilization of an alternative monetary unit unattainable, as it lacks a physical manifestation and instead thrives in the realm of the internet.

Distinct wallet systems designated for individual cryptocurrencies

You have the option to install a distinct wallet on your personal computer. This methodology unequivocally offers a secure means of preserving digital currencies, as each of these wallets confers the capability to manage the private key.

If the latter is securely stored, such as in written form or on an offline flash drive, one can possess unwavering certainty regarding the security of digital savings.

Nevertheless, this approach entails certain drawbacks. Initially, the presence of numerous disorganized wallets creates a sense of discomfort. Additionally, it is imperative for each individual to securely preserve a distinct key seed-phrase, which shall serve as their corresponding private key. As the number of digital currencies in your possession increases, it becomes imperative to memorize a corresponding multitude of distinct phrases. In the event of misplacing any of these items, the entirety of the digital currency will be irretrievably lost from its associated wallet.

Exchange

A considerable number of users have a preference for keeping altcoins within the storage facilities of stock exchanges. This is highly advantageous, considering that trading platforms provide support for a wide range of alloys, numbering in the hundreds. Nevertheless, it is important to acknowledge that you will be required to confer financial resources to a third party. The majority of cryptographic instruments exhibit centralization, being devoid of any insurance against hacking incidents, and are frequently vulnerable to Distributed Denial of Service (DDoS) attacks, thereby posing a threat to the security of funds. If you refrain from engaging in cryptocurrency trading on exchanges, it is advisable to explore alternative avenues to securely store your crypto-assets for long-term purposes.

These avenues should ideally offer private key control, enabling you to maintain absolute control over your digital assets.

Online Wallets

This alternative equally denotes the oversight of financial resources by a third party. In contrast, digital wallets available on the internet frequently offer extensive compatibility with a variety of prominent digital currencies, and additionally facilitate transactions at nominal fees.

Mobile wallets

At present, a plethora of mobile wallet applications cater to both the Android and iOS platforms. Numerous online platforms offering crypto-currencies also possess a mobile adaptation.

Certain mobile wallets exhibit a strong degree of dependability (owing to their ability to securely store the seed-phrase) and possess an intuitive user interface. For such purposes, one can consider utilizing a mobile wallet like Coinomi.

User interactions in the shape of web browser add-ons

In this particular section, Jaxx has garnered significant acclaim, serving as add-ons for the web browsers Chrome and Firefox. It encompasses user-friendliness, sleek design, and customizable settings. Furthermore, and of utmost importance, it confers upon you the authority to manage the private key through a seed-phrase.

Desktop wallets

An effective instrument is a computer-installed multicurrency wallet. For instance, Exodus exemplifies a proficient and visually appealing interface, equipped with the capability to oversee private keys and a pre-established exchange platform known as ShapeShift. Currently, the wallet is compatible with a total of 7 digital currencies, namely Ethereum (ETH), Dash (DASH), Litecoin (LTC), Augur (REP), Golem (GNT), and Dogecoin (DOGE). Regarding the Jaxx wallet, there is also a desktop iteration accessible for Windows, OS X, and Linux.

Hardware wallets

This form of cryptocurrency may be deemed the most dependable given that these devices offer optimal security through the "cold storage" of digital assets in a secure and isolated setting. This may be considered the optimal approach for the extended preservation of substantial financial resources. The hardware crypto contains a securely embedded private key, which serves the purpose of signing transactions. Commonly favored wallets of this category include Ledger Nano S, Trezor, and KeepKey. Each of them offers support for several widely-accepted alternative cryptocurrencies such as Ethereum (ETH), Litecoin (LTC), Dash, and others.

8.1. Complete the process of wallet and security registration

Which wallet should one opt for?

1. Utilize an offline wallet from a reputable source, such as the one provided at bitcoin.org, to store substantial amounts of funds for an extended duration.

2. Coinbase online wallet: Please use this link - https://goo.gl/UFXaio - if there is a need to occasionally send payments, as it has been observed that exchange platforms can be susceptible to hacking and may not be held accountable for any loss of funds. It should be noted that this recommendation is particularly

applicable for individuals actively engaged in trading activities.

Security:

Enable Two-Factor Authentication for your online wallet utilizing the following method:

Dear users, the instructions for utilizing Google Authenticator can be found at the following link: https://goo.gl/15448V.

For computers: https://goo.gl/ep0xf1

For Android: https://goo.gl/sbBxn

For iOS: https://goo.gl/ZeYgVq

Secure the offline wallet by applying an encryption method and inputting the password.

Deactivating the Internet connection, implementing antivirus software, uninstalling applications with remote access capabilities.

Embedding codes onto physical paper / creating a storage device with electronic memory.

9. Could you please explain the mechanisms employed for conducting transactions within the bitcoin network? Why has there been a significant delay in the crediting of funds?

9.1. The process of sending transactions to Bitcoin

Please provide the recipient's wallet address and specify the exact amount before sending the transaction for confirmation within the Memory Pool network.

The transaction necessitates a minimum of 3 confirmations (preferably 6 for absolute certainty that the transaction will not be cancelled) from the miners, who evaluate whether the selected transaction can be accommodated within the current maximum block size of 1 MB based on its byte size.

Once the miners have validated the transaction, it is subsequently incorporated into the blockchain and the transfer of funds to the recipient's wallet is recorded as payment.

9.2. What factors influence the expediency of payment delivery on the Bitcoin network.

Aggregate memory consumption of the Memory Pool network, encompassing the RAM utilization across all interconnected miners. As the quantity of transactions transmitted by all members to the network increases, the aggregate weight of these transactions becomes greater, resulting in a decrease in processing speed.

The transaction was excessively burdensome and it did not align with the parameters of the current block.

The transaction size may be smaller if you were to transfer 1 bitcoin in comparison to transferring the transaction to 1 bitcoin. On the other hand, the transaction size may increase if you were to receive 0.1 bitcoins, repeat this process 10 times, collect 1 bitcoin from them, and then proceed with the transaction. In the initial scenario, the magnitude of the outbound transaction will be lower compared to the latter.

What is the IoT? The centralized management of specific kinds of electronic devices, such as the supervision of ambient temperature within a storage facility, under the control of a network. Smart contracts enable the automation of the management of remote systems. The convergence of software, sensors, and the network enables the transmission of data between objects and mechanisms. The outcome enhances system efficacy and enhances cost supervision.

The leading participants in the manufacturing, technology, and telecommunications industries are all competing for supremacy in the Internet of Things (IoT) field. Consider reputable companies such as Samsung, IBM, and AT&T. IoT applications encompass a wide range of operations, spanning from the upkeep of mechanical components through predictive maintenance to the analysis of data and the management of automated systems on a large scale. This expansion is a logical progression from the current infrastructure that is overseen by established industry leaders.

Neighborhood Micro grids:

Blockchain technology facilitates the transaction of renewable energy produced by local micro grids through a decentralized marketplace. In the event that solar panels generate surplus energy, it is automatically redistributed through smart contracts based on the Ethereum platform. As the Internet of Things (IoT) continues to progress, various other applications will emerge for the implementation of comparable forms of smart contract automation.

Situated in the borough of Brooklyn, Consensys is a globally renowned organization that specializes in the development of a diverse array of applications for the Ethereum blockchain platform. A collaborative endeavor they are engaged in is the development of Trans active Grid, in conjunction with the distributed energy enterprise, LO3. A prototype initiative that is presently operational leverages Ethereum smart contracts to automate the surveillance and re-allocation of energy within micro grids. This aforementioned "intelligent grid" serves as a preliminary instance of IoT functionality.

Identity management:

There exists an indisputable requirement for enhanced identity management in the realm of the internet. The authentication of one's identity serves as the crucial factor in facilitating online financial transactions. Nonetheless, the measures to address the security vulnerabilities associated with online commerce are highly flawed. Distributed ledgers provide advanced mechanisms for establishing individual identity, coupled with the potential for digitizing personal documentation. Ensuring a robust identity is imperative when engaging in online interactions, particularly within the realm of the sharing economy. In online transactions, a favorable reputation stands as the utmost prerequisite for conducting business.

The process of formulating digital identity standards has demonstrated itself to be intricately intricate. Setting aside the technical obstacles, the establishment of a comprehensive online identification system necessitates collaboration between private corporations and governmental agencies. Additionally, when considering the necessity of managing legal frameworks across various jurisdictions, the issue becomes significantly more complex. E-Commerce conducted online presently depends on the SSL certificate (represented by the small green lock) as a means to ensure secure transactions on the internet. Netki is a fledgling company with a goal of establishing a standardized Secure Sockets Layer (SSL) protocol specifically tailored for blockchain technology. Netki, after recently disclosing a seed round of $3.5 million, anticipates the release of its product in the early months of 2017.

AML and KYC:

The potential adaptation of blockchain technology offers a promising avenue for the integration of anti-money laundering (AML) and know your customer (KYC) practices. Presently, financial establishments are faced with the need to undertake a cumbersome and intricate procedure for every prospective client. Potential avenues for curtailing KYC expenses involve implementing cross-institutional patron authentication protocols, thereby simultaneously bolstering oversight capabilities and augmenting analysis efficacy.

The company Polycoin, a startup, offers an Anti-Money Laundering (AML) and Know Your Customer (KYC) solution which entails the analysis of transactions. The transactions that are deemed suspicious are directed to the attention of the compliance officers.

Tradle, a separate startup, is currently in the process of developing an innovative application known as Trust in Motion (TiM). TiM is considered a platform akin to Instagram, specifically designed for KYC processes, where customers can conveniently capture images of essential documents such as passports and utility bills. Once verified by the bank, this data is cryptographically stored on the blockchain.

Data management:

Currently, individuals have the opportunity to avail themselves of social media platforms such as Facebook without charge, on the condition that they provide their personal information in return. In the future, individuals will be empowered to effectively oversee and market the data that their online interactions generate. Due to its inherent divisibility into smaller units, Bitcoin, or a similar digital currency, is highly probable to emerge as the preferred medium of exchange for such transactions.

The MIT project Enigma recognizes that safeguarding user privacy is an essential prerequisite for the successful establishment of a personal data marketplace. Enigma employs cryptographic methods to facilitate the partitioning of individual data sets across nodes while concurrently enabling collective computations to be executed on the entire data group. Dividing the data into fragments additionally enhances the scalability of Enigma, in contrast to blockchain solutions where data replication occurs on each individual node. A commitment has been made to deliver a Beta launch within the upcoming six months.

Land title registration:

Blockchains, serving as publicly accessible ledgers, have the potential to enhance the efficiency of various forms of record-keeping. Property titles serve as a prime illustration. They have a propensity to be vulnerable to fraudulent activities, alongside being financially burdensome and requiring significant manpower to manage.

Several nations are currently engaged in the implementation of land registry initiatives utilizing blockchain technology. In 2015, Honduras was the pioneering nation to officially declare this initiative, although the present status of the project remains ambiguous. In the course of this year, a formal agreement was established between the Republic of Georgia and the Bitfury

Group to collaboratively devise a blockchain-based platform to manage property titles. According to reports, it has been noted that Hernando de Soto, a distinguished economist renowned for his work in promoting property rights, is set to provide valuable guidance regarding the undertaking. Sweden has recently made a declaration regarding its ongoing exploration of a blockchain-based solution for managing property titles.

Stock trading:

The utilization of blockchains in stock trading demonstrates a compelling rationale due to the promising prospect of enhanced efficiency in share settlement. When implemented in a peer-to-peer manner, trade confirmations achieve near-instantaneous processing, contrasting with the traditional three-day clearance period. Potentially, this results in the elimination of intermediaries, including the clearing house, auditors, and custodians, from the process.

Several stock and commodities exchanges are currently in the process of developing and testing blockchain applications for the range of services they provide. Noteworthy examples include the ASX (Australian Securities Exchange), the Deutsche Börse (Frankfurt's stock exchange), and the JPX (Japan Exchange Group). The most notable entity in this field, largely recognized as the pioneer, is Nasdaq's Linq, which serves as a platform for conducting private market transactions, usually involving early-stage companies and investors prior to an initial public offering (IPO). Linq, in collaboration with the blockchain technology firm

Chain, unveiled the successful conclusion of its inaugural share transaction in 2015. In a more recent development, Nasdaq has made an announcement regarding the initiation of a trial blockchain project aimed at facilitating proxy voting on the esteemed Estonian Stock Market.

After grasping the above idea. I am certain that you are aware of the significant role that blockchain plays in the cryptocurrency industry.

Bitcoin Introduction

Bitcoin functions as a virtual currency, in addition to serving as a protocol and software system. It functions as a distributed digital payment system, characterized by its decentralized architecture spanning a vast network. The simultaneous functioning of these elements facilitates rapid peer-to-peer transactions, thereby allowing for global payments with negligible or nonexistent transaction processing expenses. It employs a peer-to-peer network infrastructure to circumvent the need for dependence on a centralized monetary authority for the issuance and regulation of currency. Under this system, it is not feasible to manipulate the value of bitcoins or induce inflation through excessive currency production. Additionally, access to bitcoin is available to individuals who possess a Bitcoin client.

The network itself assumes the responsibility of overseeing transactions and the generation of bitcoin, thereby enabling the regulated and decentralized creation of currency via a mechanism referred to as 'mining.' The utilization of cryptography ensures the preservation of transactional integrity. Bitcoins possess a unique characteristic wherein they uphold a singular purpose during their utilization, restricted solely to the individual possessing ownership rights. Conventional monetary systems incorporate regulatory bodies for monitoring and oversight, whereas Bitcoin lacks such governance structures.

Bitcoin presently represents a realm within the burgeoning global economy characterized by immense potential, intricate complexities, and considerable volatility. Due to the nascent stage of Bitcoin, this will remain a prevailing circumstance for the foreseeable future. At present, it is employed as a means of digital payment. In terms of efficiency, it surpasses all alternative methods for transmitting and receiving funds. The functionality of the system renders PayPal as having a dated and cumbersome interface. However, its potential surpasses initial expectations significantly. It aims to emerge as a formidable competitor to all existing national currencies. Certainly, there is a possibility that it may replace them in the future. Cryptocurrencies, prominently Bitcoin, possess the capacity to revolutionize the realms of currency and finance, contingent upon the voluntary adoption by individuals, rather than coercive implementation enforced by governments. Currently, nevertheless, the main beneficiaries and proponents of this nascent digital currency are individuals from the younger cohort who have come of age in an era marked by the ubiquity of computer programming.

Please observe the advancements made in digital innovation during the past few years. In the past two decades, there has been a significant transformation in communication methods. Traditional letters have given way to the emergence of emails, while television has undergone a transition into the digital realm, exemplified by platforms like YouTube. Similarly, telephone technology has advanced remarkably, shifting from the era of wall-mounted units to portable video phones that can fit in our pockets. The advent of the digital revolution can be attributed to the free market rather than the government. It wasn't an easy plan to begin with. Conversely, it arose as a consequence of experimentation and refinement within the realm of commercial trade.

Bitcoin finds itself in a comparable predicament to that of electronic mail during the 1990s. No one could provide an explanation regarding its functioning or justifications for its necessity. A significant proportion of the email addresses consisted of lengthy numerical combinations, with a limited selection of commercial services being accessible. In order to facilitate message transmission and reception, a dial-up connection was required. Nonetheless, in the event of server disruptions, operations would abruptly halt due to the absence of a contingency plan for immediate restoration. Due to a lack of familiarity with email usage, individuals encountered difficulties in effectively composing messages, resulting in awkward correspondence. During that period, the prevalence of spam problems and the rampant proliferation of viruses significantly plagued this digital medium, causing a nightmarish experience.

Throughout the various stages of email's development, there was a pervasive skepticism regarding its potential usefulness. There were assertions made that the letter would never be susceptible to replacement. We were apprised of the hazardous nature of the situation, and it was deemed burdensome by individuals. However, gradually and systematically, nearly every impediment associated with email was resolved as time elapsed. The advancement of technology met a standstill, leading people to realize a fundamental truth regarding software. That particular technology showcases remarkable intelligence and sustains its excellence, notwithstanding the gradual stabilization and consolidation of the services that utilize it.

Undoubtedly, email emerged as the prevailing mode of communication and is presently deemed the most convenient platform for correspondence. Emerging developments in communication technologies, such as Facebook and Skype messaging, as well as smartphone SMS systems, are achieving significant strides. Portable electronic devices that offer navigational guidance and real-time traffic information aid us in traversing our surroundings. All of this is now commonly accepted without question. The circumstances haven't always been as they are currently. Nevertheless, it has become an undeniable reality in contemporary society. It does not receive any further consideration from anyone.

The subsequent phase in this progression is apparent: there is a necessity for the reimagining of currency. For the past century, the government and the central bank have successfully assumed control over the currency known as the dollar. Currently, there exists a market demand for financial assets that shift away from governmental control and embrace the paradigm of digitalization. It is imperative for it to be liberated from the control of a politically designated central bank and returned to the possession of the populace.

Thus far, Bitcoin has been recognized as the most prosperous endeavor in establishing such a currency. It is supported by a myriad of venture capital investments from Silicon Valley. Youths employ this platform as a means of economizing, while others go to the extent of leveraging it as a source of income. It has been extensively covered in a prominent feature story by each renowned newspaper. It is becoming increasingly popular and lucrative for websites that offer support for it. It offers a sanctuary for nations grappling with economic challenges, and its adoption by merchants continues to grow steadily.

Upon its initial introduction in 2009, numerous individuals derided and made dire predictions of its inevitable downfall. It garnered extensive coverage in prominent financial publications four years hence. Every passing moment witnesses the occurrence of financial transactions, as an increasing number of individuals engage in the movement of substantial sums of money on a daily basis. The market sector, in its entirety, possesses a market valuation that exceeds $1 billion, a figure that, although minuscule within the global financial landscape, significantly surpasses all prognostications.

Neither a politician nor a commission had any involvement in the creation or approval of Bitcoin. It is not subject to regulation by any central bank, and there exist no political or administrative deficiencies in its management. The sole determinant of its success is the market. The market's main determining factor lies in the absence of any singular corporation that possesses ownership or control over it. Its valuation remains unaltered by prevailing currencies, with the aim of serving as the primary standard of measurement.

Bitcoin offers an alternative to regulatory measures imposed on monetary systems. Upon the conversion of dollars into Bitcoins, the means of exchange becomes detached from the purview of the Federal Reserve. This carries significant implications for the formulation of monetary policy. In summary, should bitcoin's potential be realized. There is a possibility that we are witnessing the emergence of a novel international currency that could effectively rival, if not entirely supplant, the government's unsuccessful endeavor with fiat currency. In the event of its failure, the Bitcoin experiment will serve as a catalyst for other endeavors aiming to establish digital currency units that are traded openly, instead of being dependent on governmental control.

In order to achieve a thorough understanding of Bitcoin, it is essential to acknowledge that its purpose does not revolve around serving as an investment instrument. The proposed innovation is industrially motivated and akin to significant advancements such as the steam engine, railroad, steel industry, or electronic mail. The crux of the matter pertains to software. It is derived from a cryptographic principle. The technology it is utilizing is in the process of developing into a legitimate payment system for monetary transactions. Its most notable utilization currently lies in the transmission of funds from one individual to another. It is as uncomplicated as engaging in text-based communication on a mobile device.

Nevertheless, all technologies are introduced into society through the medium of the commercial economy. Speculative elements will invariably be part of its evolutionary process. Errors, unexpected occurrences, unsuccessful attempts, and obstacles are all inherent aspects of the market, alongside advancements, achievements, and, in the end, heightened human gratification. In the interim, a significant number of individuals will perceive Bitcoin and other digital currencies as a means to achieve rapid wealth accumulation. A significant number of individuals will amass substantial wealth, while a considerable number of individuals will experience unemployment. By contrast, who, instead, will perceive the broader perspective? The field of economic history exhibits a discernible inclination. On a daily basis, the inclination to establish a contemporary alternative to government-issued currency gains momentum. There will be no halting the progress of a technology that has surpassed its utility.

Bitcoin: A Summary

Satoshi Nakamoto conceptualized Bitcoin, an innovative payment system which he unveiled in 2008 and subsequently introduced as open-source software in 2009. Due to the decentralized structure of the system, users have the ability to directly interact with one another without the need for an intermediary. Transactions are validated by network nodes and subsequently recorded in a publicly distributed ledger called the blockchain. The ledger possesses its own form of currency, widely recognized as bitcoin. The decentralized nature of the virtual currency system is acknowledged by the US Treasury, as there is neither a central repository nor a sole administrator. Despite the presence of preexisting systems, Bitcoin is commonly recognized as the initial cryptocurrency.

Bitcoin is renowned as the globe's inaugural form of decentralized digital currency. With regards to the overall market valuation, it holds the distinction of being the largest in its category. Bitcoins serve the purpose of verifying and documenting transactions on a publicly-accessible ledger, while individuals contribute their computational resources in exchange for these digital assets. The activity in question is referred to as mining, where individuals, known as miners, receive compensation in the form of transaction fees and newly created bitcoins. Bitcoins can be acquired through the exchange of different currencies, commodities, and services, in addition to the process of mining. Users have the option to send and receive bitcoins by paying a transaction fee.

Bitcoin Philosophy

Temporarily, let us set aside the technological aspects of Bitcoin; what sets it apart is its distinctiveness in not necessitating a central entity for the production of currency units or the validation of transactions. Due to the distributed nature of the system, these global decisions are implicitly and democratically determined by the system's users. The subsequent pair of illustrations can be employed to showcase a general understanding of the system's functionality:

Individuals are granted bitcoins as a form of compensation for actively engaging in the network. Conversely, it is not possible for users to manipulate the system in order to enhance their incentives, as they are required to personally validate the awards. Consequently, in the event that a user attempts to discreetly enhance their reward, the other users will not permit it.

User A employs Bitcoin A as the medium for executing a payment transaction towards user B. Bitcoin transactions are made public in order to hinder user A from employing bitcoin A to carry out a transaction with a third-party user C. Upon the second transaction being detected by the rest of the network, it shall decline authorization, thereby averting A's ability to reuse bitcoin A a second time.

Consequently, it is the users who assume the responsibility of making decisions that are conventionally undertaken by a central monetary authority. This characteristic sets Bitcoin apart as a form of currency that embodies democratic principles. The progression of the system is shaped by the majority of public aspirations, as is customary in all democratic societies. Nevertheless, "one user = one vote" does not have an equivalent in this context as the distribution of weights within the system is contingent upon the computer power each user contributes to the network. In the context of Bitcoin, a more precise statement would be that the allocation of computing power directly corresponds to the proportion of voting influence. Consequently, provided that the majority of the network's processing power remains under the control of honest users, the network will develop in accordance with their desired trajectory. The concept at hand could be framed as a form of "unequal democracy," where the level of a user's engagement in the system dictates the guiding principle.

When considered from this perspective, Bitcoin embodies an entirely novel economic and social paradigm. If Bitcoin or a comparable system were to be adopted, the regulation of currency growth would not be carried out directly by governments and financial institutions. Indeed, it is true that legislation can potentially exert indirect influence; however, it does not possess any authority to dictate or regulate its conduct. Due to the inherent global nature of electronic currency, effective regulation of such a form of payment would pose significant challenges.

Moreover, given that these circumstances have not been observed in the realm of economic theory, the ramifications of the widespread integration and utilization of bitcoin remain uncertain.

If you find yourself uncertain about initiating a blog or if you have recently embarked on this endeavor, please allow me to elucidate why your choice to commence your very own blog is indeed commendable, or if you are on the verge of doing so. It is widely recognized by discerning readers that blogging constitutes a highly innovative means of articulating and conveying one's thoughts. I recollect having commenced my blog with the intention of aiding individuals and articulating my perspectives through the medium of the internet.

Luckily, blogging proved to be instrumental in satisfying my requirements. It facilitated the articulation of my perspectives in a manner consistent with my intentions, and significantly enhanced my capacity for innovation. The initial topic of my first blog pertained to the realm of generating income via the internet. Fondly, I recall the month when I published said blog, during which my website garnered approximately 180 visitors. While this may not be considered substantial traffic by certain individuals, for a novice attempting to convey his thoughts through written words, it can undeniably be characterized as an achievement, if nothing else.

Honestly, the primary motivation behind the establishment of this blog was to enhance the visibility of my business and generate sales. Additionally, I had a keen interest in enhancing the reach and influence of my brand, as well as disseminating my expertise within the specific industry I had specialized in. I was previously unaware that it is possible to generate income through the medium of blogs until a few months into my venture. While establishing connections with individuals online, I was advised by a fellow blogger to incorporate Google Adsense into my blog in order to generate a financial gain. Therefore, I decided to heed his advice.

After a few months had elapsed, I had already started to generate a modest level of traffic to my blog. Subsequently, upon initiating the utilization of paid advertisements on my blog, I experienced the commencement of monetary gains. I vividly recollect the exhilaration I felt upon receiving my initial payment, which amounted to $100. This was my initial experience of earning money through the internet, subsequently resulting in a feeling of enthusiasm.

Over the course of several months, my blog experienced gradual expansion and subsequently generated increased revenue. Unbeknownst to me, I would eventually derive financial gains from a digital platform that I initially employed solely for the purpose of advertising my business. Currently, I am generating a monthly income of over $1,000 through my blog. Although it may not be a substantial amount, I am generating income without any expenses, all the while promoting my business.

Subsequently, I was contacted by a company who expressed interest in having me endorse their product through a blog post, and they offered me a compensation of $400 for this promotional initiative. Upon reflecting, it occurred to me that if I continue to receive leads on a bi-monthly basis, I would have the potential to effortlessly earn $2,000 per month by simply crafting comprehensive 3,000-word explanations outlining the product's capabilities and providing my informed perspective on it. Honestly, I must admit that I am increasingly developing a fondness for this blogging endeavor. I have successfully established an online revenue stream, thereby achieving the aspiration many individuals strive for.

Following one year of engaging in the practice of blogging, I encountered a concept known as affiliate marketing. For individuals who may be unfamiliar with the concept of affiliate marketing, it is essentially a form of compensation received in the event that a product is purchased through a hyperlink provided by the affiliate. The precise words that came to mind were, "Given the considerable amount of traffic my blog attracts, it seems sensible to augment my earnings." In hindsight, it was undoubtedly the correct choice. In the span of just a few months, I experienced a substantial increase in my monthly earnings, transitioning from $2,000 to nearly $15,000, by embarking on an affiliate marketing venture, leveraging the influx of visitors to my blog.

What initially began as a straightforward means of promoting my business has transformed into a source of income significant enough for me to consider relinquishing my business entirely. Blogging not only furnished me with a medium to articulate my thoughts and further advance my business, but significantly enabled me to earn my livelihood.

For individuals who are new to this endeavor and are considering discontinuing or refraining from engaging in the practice of blogging as a whole, I would like to pose a question: Are you desirous of establishing connections with others, sharing your unique ideas and perspectives, all while simultaneously achieving noteworthy financial success? If your response is in the affirmative, proceed to establish your blog either immediately or subsequent to the completion of perusing this publication. If the answer is negative, kindly distribute this book to an individual commencing a blog.

Please be advised that I acknowledge the difficulty one may face in reaching a decision to commence, nevertheless, once that choice is made, it becomes irreversible. By promptly seizing the opportunity at hand and not deferring it for another year, you shall expeditiously embark upon the path leading to the life you aspire to lead. After several years of dedicated blogging, I have successfully established my blog as a sustainable source of income, proving it to be the most advantageous decision I have made thus far.

To be candid, it is unnecessary to allocate your time towards a conventional 9-5 job just to secure financial resources and await the arrival of the weekend. I assert without any hesitation that engaging in blogging is an advantageous means to swiftly generate income and sustain a livelihood communally with one's professional pursuits. By adhering to the prescribed procedures outlined in this published work, one will achieve the desired outcome at a faster pace compared to my own experience.

Niche

Selecting a niche is arguably one of the foremost factors that necessitate contemplation when embarking on the initiation of your blog. A recommended approach to selecting a niche for your blog would involve identifying all of your interests and activities that you enjoy engaging in during your leisure time. Is the activity in question associated with fishing or skateboarding? It is imperative that the subject matter chosen for your blog is one that resonates deeply with your personal passion, as this genuine enthusiasm will be evident in your writing. If one lacks interest in the subject matter of their blog, they are likely to receive less traffic compared to a blog on a topic of genuine interest.

At this juncture, it is evident that the selection of an appropriate niche holds significant significance. Upon selecting the appropriate niche that aligns authentically with your personality and character, we can proceed. Subsequently, when you have made a definitive choice regarding the niche in which your blog will be centered, it is imperative to conduct a more thorough examination of it.

In the role of a blog writer, it is crucial to thoroughly familiarize yourself with the domain you will be writing about. This fundamental measure is indispensable, as it will greatly contribute to your triumph in attracting and engaging your target audience. If you have indeed adhered to the initial step of selecting a niche that aligns with your existing passion, it would consequently facilitate your access to pertinent information pertaining to the latest news and developments within that niche. Despite this, there exist several approaches to comprehensively explore and obtain exhaustive information pertaining to your niche, which we shall delve into in the current chapter.

To be more precise, our focus will revolve around exploring three methodologies for comprehensively acquiring knowledge about your niche, enabling you to remain informed about current trends and emerging subjects. To gain a deeper understanding of your niche, it would be advantageous to utilize social media fan pages that disseminate pertinent information and updates. The second approach entails familiarizing oneself with the foremost blogs in your area of expertise, while the third entails acquiring a deeper understanding of the historical aspects pertaining to your specific niche, as I will elucidate the ways in which it can prove beneficial.

Social media

Currently, social media stands as one of the foremost influential means to remain connected with the latest developments in the online realm. Particularly in the context of niche subjects, it is widely acknowledged that the general populace increasingly depends on social media platforms to stay abreast of the most current news, as opposed to traditional mediums such as newspapers or televised news channels. While I don't assert that newspapers or news channels are obsolete or lacking in value, it is often the case that social media platforms relay news to us more swiftly than any news channel or newspaper could.

Indeed, it is a matter of common knowledge that the majority of bloggers find it imperative to remain current with the latest news and trends by utilizing social media as their medium of choice. Presently, I would like to bring your attention to three prominent platforms in the realm of social media that I believe would be advantageous for you to utilize. The initial recommendation would be the widely recognized website known as Facebook. It is common knowledge that Facebook is a leading and widely recognized social media platform. In the event that there are any topics or information pertaining to your specific industry or area of interest, Facebook will provide you with news and updates. A viable alternative would be to utilize Instagram, and I strongly advise employing Instagram as a means to remain abreast of any pertinent information or disputes within your specific sphere of interest.

Lastly, I would suggest employing Snapchat as an additional social media platform. In recent times, Snapchat has commenced utilizing its platform to furnish users with news and updates pertaining to an extensive range of highly specialized topics. To be candid, the quality of the stories is less than satisfactory, but occasionally, they effectively stimulate active thinking and promote further investigation into a particular subject. With that being said, let us now delve into the particulars regarding how these three platforms can be utilized to your benefit.

Let's first discuss Facebook. At present, Facebook boasts approximately 2.27 billion active users, thereby providing a comprehensive repository of news and real-time trends across a vast range of subjects. To elucidate further, if your objective is to acquire deeper insights into your specialized field and stay updated on its current tendencies, it is advisable to partake in fan pages associated with your niche. Facebook possesses an extensive array of fan pages encompassing various niches, alleviating any concerns by ensuring that one will discover a fan page pertinent to their own niche. The purpose of establishing a Facebook fan page is to deliver the most recent information and updates pertaining to the specific field or interest to one's followers. It is highly recommended to utilize this platform to your benefit.

Instagram is a widely acknowledged platform in current times. Gradually, yet steadily, Instagram is emerging as the preeminent social media platform, poised to surpass Facebook in prominence. The reason is simple. The reason behind its popularity lies in its enjoyable and simplistic nature. Much like Facebook, a plethora of fan pages catering to every conceivable niche can be found. Utilize this instrument to remain abreast of the latest trends and subjects pertaining to your specific industry.

Furthermore, our next topic of discussion will revolve around the social media platform commonly referred to as Snapchat. Some individuals among you may possess familiarity with this particular social media platform, which predominantly serves as a platform for numerous users to actively engage in the sharing of photographs captured by their own devices. Snapchat boasts a functionality referred to as "the story," which is primarily employed for the straightforward purpose of featuring content on the Snapchat platform. The purpose of this platform is to offer users with the most recent news and updates; however, it should be noted that the specialized section is comparatively less extensive than that of a platform like Facebook. Furthermore, as alluded to earlier, it stimulates cognitive activity. The categories encompassed on Snapchat are considerably wide, albeit being a comparatively recent addition; it would therefore be unrealistic to anticipate it to rival the platforms of Facebook and Instagram.

Alterations To The Bitcoin Value System

When Bitcoin was initially introduced as a form of digital currency, being one of the pioneering ones, its value was meager. Numerous individuals held reservations about its sustainability, with some harboring concerns over potential financial losses associated with their investments. However, there were individuals who harbored faith in the concept and chose to allocate their resources towards its development. Those individuals exhibited astute judgment, as the modest amount they allocated to their investment in Bitcoin merely eight years ago has now surged in value significantly. For a nominal sum, they have transformed into individuals of great affluence.

Year 2009

The mean value of the Bitcoin price is .0001 US Dollars.

If an individual were to possess a total of 10 Bitcoin, their value would amount to

.001 Bitcoin, which is equivalent to less than one cent.

Length of market presence: None

The initial investors in Bitcoin made relatively modest financial commitments. Indeed, individuals who made a financial commitment of 10 dollars in reality obtained 100,000 units of Bitcoin. At that particular point in time, their awareness was lacking with regard to the eventual substantial financial gains that would be witnessed.

During that period, a sum of 10 dollars would have afforded a significant volume of Bitcoin. However, individuals who harbored genuine faith in the underlying concept of Bitcoin went on to invest far more substantial amounts than a mere 10 dollars. Certain individuals have allocated substantial sums, ranging from hundreds to thousands of dollars, towards their investments in Bitcoin. Unbeknownst to them, their actions inadvertently contributed to the appreciation of Bitcoin's value and spurred its price inflation.

Year 2010

The mean value of Bitcoin stands at 0.07 United States dollars.

If one were to possess 10 units of Bitcoin, they would possess approximately 0.7 units of Bitcoin, equating to slightly less than one dollar.

Length of time in the market: 1 year

This marked the onset of numerous substantial surges in the value of Bitcoin within the preceding eight years. The initial value was significantly below one cent, and the price subsequently escalated due to the involvement of investors and individuals seeking to partake in the Bitcoin market. This is the juncture at which numerous individuals perceived that Bitcoin might not be the subject of mockery after all. Although the price of seven cents may seem insignificant, especially when compared to other investment options available in the market, it constituted a substantial increase.

Astute investors recognized this and consequently augmented their investments in Bitcoin. On numerous occasions, the typical acquisition of Bitcoin encompassed a substantial sum of thousands of dollars. The individuals involved in this endeavor were not renowned investors, but rather technology enthusiasts who aspired to participate in the opportunities presented.

However, currently, if you happen to have an extra sum of 10 dollars, you would be able to acquire a total of 142 Bitcoin. Individuals who engaged in such activities during that particular period demonstrated wisdom.

Year 2011

The mean value of Bitcoin is $15 USD.

If an individual were to possess 10 Bitcoin, their ownership would amount to a value of 150 dollars.

Duration of presence in the market: 2 years

This marked the second instance within the timeline of Bitcoin in which it experienced a substantial surge in value. It was driven by investors who allocated substantial funds to enter the Bitcoin market, providing them with the opportunity to amass significant wealth in the future.

At this juncture, it dawned upon a majority of investors that Bitcoin had established a permanent presence within the market. They were aware that it held tremendous potential to revolutionize the functioning of the stock market and stood poised to become one of the most rapidly expanding investment prospects globally.

Year 2012

Mean value of Bitcoin: Seven United States Dollars

If you were in possession of 10 Bitcoin, the value of your assets would amount to 70 dollars of Bitcoin.

Duration of market presence: 3 years.

In a significant departure from its brief chronicle, Bitcoin experienced a decline in value for the inaugural occasion. In light of its limited tenure in the market, it comes as no surprise that Bitcoin experienced a significant decline, albeit relatively substantial when juxtaposed against its previous remarkable growth.

Indeed, the price point of $7 was regarded by many as the maximum threshold at which Bitcoin was expected to reach its peak.

People initiated the process of withdrawing. They divested their Bitcoin holdings due to concerns regarding potential future depreciation.

The astute investors, however, were aware of the recurrent pattern of a decline in price preceding a substantial upswing. They retained ownership of the Bitcoin. They persevered and their steadfastness with regards to the market they opted to enter proved to be highly advantageous.

Year 2013

The mean price of Bitcoin is $100 in terms of US currency.

If you were in possession of 10 units of Bitcoin, you would possess a total value of 1,000 dollars in Bitcoin.

Number of years in circulation: 4.

Individuals who maintained their Bitcoin holdings amidst the decline in value were overjoyed, as they were fully aware that their decision to retain their

Bitcoin was astute and prudent. It was imperative for them to retain it, as it facilitated the acquisition of a significantly larger quantity of Bitcoin.

Although the individuals in question believed that their abundance of Bitcoin granted them blessings, those fortunate enough to have acquired it in 2009 were in a far superior position. Had you invested 10 dollars in Bitcoin in 2009, you would have achieved millionaire status by 2013. In fact, there were several individuals who reached that juncture. A considerable number of individuals opted to withdraw their funds at that juncture, content with achieving a million in profits and desiring to exit prior to incurring any losses. Still, others stayed. Several individuals believed that the situation could not deteriorate beyond the initial investment of 10 dollars.

Year 2014

The mean value of Bitcoin is calculated to be 600 US dollars.

If an individual were to possess 10 Bitcoin, their holdings would amount to a value of 6,000 dollars in Bitcoin.

Duration of presence in the market: 5 years.

This constituted an additional increment, albeit not of significant magnitude, analogous to the initial stages. Although comparatively smaller in scale, the increase was substantial, catapulting individuals who had invested during the Bitcoin selling season in 2009 into the realm of multimillionaires.

Once again, there was an increased number of individuals who liquidated their Bitcoin holdings. They desired to depart prior to the point of irrevocability. This statement held particularly true for individuals who had substantial financial interests in the realm of millions of dollars.

Year 2015

The mean value of Bitcoin currently stands at 220 US dollars.

If you possessed a total of 10 Bitcoin, the corresponding value would amount to 2,200 dollars.

Duration of presence in the market: 6 years

During this period, authorities undertook the closure and seizure of the illicit online marketplace known as the Silk Road. It was a period that inflicted significant harm upon individuals whose sole focus revolved around Bitcoin transactions, consequently provoking a decline in its value.

The experienced investors anticipated the inevitable occurrence and refrained from allowing it to impede their investment decisions. They expressed their intention to sustain their profitability from Bitcoin and proceeded accordingly. They chose to retain their Bitcoin holdings in their wallets despite the decline in value and refrained from engaging in selling activities. They expressed aspirations for its resurgence.

2016

The mean value of the Bitcoin price stands at $1,146 in US currency.

If an individual possessed a total of 10 Bitcoin, they would own Bitcoin with a market value equivalent to 11,460 dollars.

Duration of presence in the market: 7 years.

After a prolonged period, Bitcoin witnessed a surge in value, exceeding threefold for the first time in a substantial duration. Individuals who had purchased Bitcoin valued at 10 dollars in 2009 subsequently possessed a digital wallet of a significant worth exceeding one hundred thousand dollars. However, it should be noted that individuals who had purchased a substantial number of shares during the year 2009 had indeed invested substantial sums of money in Bitcoin. In terms of their financial achievements, the year 2016 marked a momentous occasion for them as they successfully surpassed the billion dollar threshold. While the individuals possess diversified holdings in distinct financial portfolios, their combined net worth remains in the billionaire range.

2017

The mean value of Bitcoin stands at 992 US dollars (as of January).

If you were in possession of 10 Bitcoin, the value of your holdings would amount to approximately 9,920 dollars' worth of Bitcoin.

Duration in the industry: 8 years.

Although there was a slight decline in the early part of the year, it is anticipated that Bitcoin will surpass the price of gold in the upcoming months. It is anticipated that the price will remain in the vicinity of $1,000 for several months before undergoing a substantial increase, approaching the $2,000 threshold.

The precise figure cannot be ascertained, however, several individuals anticipate that Bitcoin will surpass a value of $10,000 by the onset of 2020.

If you have yet to do so, the present moment presents an opportune time to invest in Bitcoin, so as to reap potential financial rewards in the future.

Potential Challenges Encountered Within The Ethereum Ecosystem

Irrespective of the nature of the subject matter, the advent of novelty is inevitably accompanied by obstacles that impede the progress. These difficulties will impede the users' ability to exert control over the platform and its software. Nevertheless, once you have comprehended the obstacles impeding your progress, you will possess the capacity to circumvent them and seamlessly carry on utilizing the system, rendering these challenges virtually inconsequential.

The initial obstacle that will come to your attention is the issue of Ethereum's scalability. Due to the frequently reiterated assertions pertaining to the operation of conventional payment network procedures, it is expected that approximately two thousand transactions shall be accomplished per second, whereas the Ethereum network, conversely, will possess a capacity limited to just seven transactions. However, you will be afforded the opportunity to modify the limit parameters, allowing you to accomplish a higher volume of transactions per second. There exists a likelihood that Ethereum may grow excessively in scale, thereby compelling users to operate complete nodes. However, in the event of an entire node being downgraded, it will result in certain businesses being the sole entities capable of procuring the necessary resources required to operate said node. Therefore, it follows that there is no necessity to download the blockchain for certain Ethereum operations.

Hence, the primary concern lies in the creation of a blockchain framework that can effectively preserve the security measures provided by Ethereum. This framework must guarantee the scalability of powerful nodes dedicated to facilitating a high volume of completed transactions.

Several additional issues that can lead to scaling problems include:

What is the current quantity of users connected to the network?

Individuals employing dedicated hardware or non-specialized hardware. When the equipment possesses specialization, its capabilities will surpass that of a non-specialized device.

The likelihood that a majority of users will utilize non-specialized hardware.

In certain instances, blocks necessitate a majority of fifty-one percent of the network's hashing power in order to effectively invalidate a transaction. However, the proposed resolution suggests that transactions could be subject to nominal fees, resulting in a diminished level of security. This will necessitate users to refrain from situations wherein an assailant on the network can opportunistically exploit a limited set of transactions to derive financial gain.

The majority of circumstances will facilitate the preservation of the attributes that contribute to the generalization of the account's blockchain. Nevertheless, the responses will be tailored to the digital currency as well as the domain's registrations or any other specialized scenarios that meet the criteria.

The matter of Ethereum will also entail challenges pertaining to time stamping. Typically, a new block is generated every ten minutes. However, if a block is constructed on a daily basis, the efficiency of the system will be compromised. Conversely, if blocks are produced at an excessively rapid rate, the platform will become inundated, resulting in performance-related challenges. This is why it is essential to maintain a balanced approach, ensuring the timely creation of blocks while preserving the optimal functioning of the system.

Hence, the primary concern will pertain to the establishment of an efficient distribution mechanism necessitating an incentive-compatible framework. This necessitates the implementation of an additional layer atop the block or chain to ensure precise timekeeping.

Additional difficulties related to time stamping will include:

Any user employing a timepiece to track standard distributions around the universally accepted real-time will encounter a deviation of twenty seconds.

It is an incontrovertible reality that the temporal interval between two nodes, in relation to the duration required for a message to be transmitted from one node to another and subsequently received, always exceeds a duration of twenty seconds.

There may exist resolutions that depend on the preexisting nodes. However, the implementation of this practice necessitates the verification of stake or the imposition of a non-Sybil token.

Several users have made the suggestion that the system will display a time that is at least one hundred and twenty seconds earlier than the internal clock of the system. This will encompass approximately ninety-nine percent of the participating nodes, compelling them to perform their necessary tasks. Please be advised that this will entail the necessity for the system to maintain self-consistency within a period of one hundred and ninety seconds.

The system will henceforth operate autonomously, eliminating the necessity of users providing proof of work.

The efficacy of the external system will be contingent upon the newly developed system. This implies that, regardless of the motive, it will remain impervious to manipulation by an assailant seeking to gain control over twenty-five percent of the network's nodes.

You may encounter various other factors that could pose challenges in your utilization of the Ethereum platform. The system developers are diligently striving to eliminate obstacles and enhance the system's user-friendliness. However, it will not rectify the issue immediately. Occasionally, there may arise complications within the system itself, which the developers may not always have the means to rectify.

Developers often overlook issues that users inevitably discover. Therefore, in the event that an issue is detected, it is imperative that it be promptly communicated and documented for inclusion in the developers' knowledge base, ensuring that it receives the necessary attention and resolution. By informing us of any issues, you will contribute to the improvement of the system for not only yourself but also for other users.

As you are aware, it is imperative to report any identified issues as the developers actively seek to address problems that are brought to their attention by users. It is imperative to bear in mind that software developers, like everyone else, are human beings who possess their own personal lives to manage alongside their professional responsibilities. The Ethereum platform comprises a substantial amount of code, which necessitates a comprehensive scrutiny in order to effectively address any issues with precision. It is inevitable that there will be problems that arise and persist for an extended duration. Therefore, place your trust in the developers, as they will successfully overcome the reported issues, resulting in an enhanced platform efficiency, all thanks to the invaluable contributions of users such as yourself.

Cryptocurrency Wallets And Storage Solutions

Cryptocurrency wallets are software applications specifically developed for the purpose of securely storing cryptocurrencies. These wallets operate in a similar manner to your personal bank account, where your fiat currency is securely stored. Cryptographic wallets enable the reception and storage of cryptocurrencies from individuals, and facilitate the transfer of digital assets as payments or conversions into conventional currencies such as the United States Dollar.

Cryptocurrency wallets are compatible with mobile devices, desktop computers, physical storage devices such as USB drives, or accessible via the internet, enabling global access from any geographical location.

There exist four primary categories of cryptocurrency wallets. These options encompass a software wallet, web wallet (alternatively referred to as a hosted wallet), hardware wallet, and a paper wallet. Among these wallets, hardware wallets are widely regarded as the most reliable means of storing digital coins and tokens due to their offline nature, which effectively prevents unauthorized access by hackers.

A hardware wallet generally refers to a USB device that is designed with a proprietary security system capable of securely storing an individual's private keys. Hardware wallets additionally provide the benefit of expedited payment processing.

Hardware wallets additionally provide advanced security technologies and consistently implement encryption measures. Consequently, in the event of your wallet being stolen, the perpetrator will be unable to gain access to your private keys.

With that being stated, presented herewith are a selection of the foremost hardware wallets currently available in the market:

Ledger Nano S

The Ledger Nano S stands out as an exceptional hardware wallet available in the market today. The storage system provides an aesthetically streamlined design, an interface that facilitates ease of use, and comprehensive backing for a variety of prevalent cryptocurrencies such as Bitcoin, Ethereum, Bitcoin Cash, Litecoin, Bitcoin Gold, Ethereum Classic, Zcash, Dogecoin, Ripple, Dash, and several others.

Users of the Ledger Nano S have the ability to visually examine and verify transactions through the device's display. Furthermore, during the device setup process, users have the option to select a personal identification number (PIN). Furthermore, individuals have the option of employing a 24-word seed to derive unique private keys for their digital currencies. Moreover, the Ledger Nano S can be seamlessly integrated with software wallets such as Mycellium, CoPay, and even MyEtherWallet.

Trezor

Any comprehensive conversation regarding hardware wallets would be remiss without acknowledging the significance of Trezor. This is attributed to the fact that the Trezor wallet stands out as one of the most enduring and highly secure hardware wallets available in the market. The wallet is regarded as an exemplar of secure and dependable storage mechanisms within the realm of cryptocurrency. Even in the event of a compromised computer's security, users still have the capability to securely authorize transactions.

Moreover, the Trezor wallet presents additional advantages, encompassing the option to seamlessly integrate it with various wallets like MetaMask, Mycellium, and MyEtherWallet. The Trezor wallet is available in two models: Trezor One and Trezor Model T. Both models have the capacity to accommodate a maximum of 689 cryptocurrencies, encompassing notable ones like Bitcoin, Litecoin, Ethereum, Bitcoin Cash, Zcash, Ethereum Classic, Dash, Namecoin, and Dogecoin, among others.

KeepKey
KeepKey serves as an additional dependable hardware wallet option. The wallet provides comparable functionalities to those of the Ledger Nano S and is compatible with all major operating systems. This implies that KeepKey is compatible with all major operating systems, namely Windows, Linux, and Macintosh, thereby enabling its use on any computer. KeepKey is additionally available as a Chrome extension, conveniently deployable from the Chrome Web Store. A significant limitation associated with KeepKey is its substantial size and bulkiness.

During the initial setup process, individuals have the option to generate a 24-word seed in an offline state. This task is conveniently facilitated by the implementation of a 3.12-inch screen, which significantly simplifies the setup process. An additional feature that you will find advantageous in the KeepKey wallet is its incorporation of ShapeShift integration, granting users the ability to access a vast array of up to 500 distinct trading pairs.

KeepKey offers compatibility for a wide range of 36 diverse cryptocurrencies, encompassing notable examples such as Bitcoin, Ethereum, Litecoin, Bitcoin Cash, Dogecoin, Dash, Aragon, and Augur, among others.

CoolWallet S
CoolWallet S is renowned as one of the most robust and reliable Bitcoin wallets available for Android and iOS platforms. The device purports to be the "initial hardware wallet incorporating an integrated exchange." This implies that it functions as a hybrid, fulfilling the dual purposes of serving as a storage medium for coins as well as facilitating trade.

The CoolWallet S boasts a form factor resembling a credit card, rendering it effortlessly stowable within a standard wallet. Regarding its physical appearance, it ranks among the most elegant hardware wallets available in the market.

The CoolWallet S is compatible with various cryptocurrencies, including Bitcoin, Litecoin, Ethereum, Ripple, Bitcoin Cash, and ERC-20 tokens. In order to establish a connection between the CoolWallet S and a mobile device, it is necessary to procure the corresponding software application from reputable mobile platforms such as Apple's App Store and Google Play store.

www.ingramcontent.com/pod-product-compliance
Lightning Source LLC
Chambersburg PA
CBHW071642210326
41597CB00017B/2083